WORKING TOGETHER

WORKING TOGETHER

55 Team Games

Lorraine L. Ukens

JOSSEY-BASS/PFEIFFER
A Wiley Company
www.pfeiffer.com

Published by

JOSSEY-BASS/PFEIFFER
A Wiley Company
989 Market Street
San Francisco, CA 94103-1741
415.433.1740; Fax 415.433.0499
800.274.4434; Fax 800.569.0443

www.pfeiffer.com

Jossey-Bass/Pfeiffer is a registered trademark of John Wiley & Sons, Inc.

ISBN: 0-7879-0354-X
Library of Congress Catalog Card Number 96-070224

Printed in the United States of America

Printing 10 9 8 7 6

We at Jossey-Bass strive to use the most environmentally sensitive paper stocks available to us. Our publications are printed on acid-free recycled stock whenever possible, and our paper always meets or exceeds minimum GPO and EPA requirements.

Contents

Introduction

The use of teams has emerged as the logical approach to sharpening an organization's competitive edge. Although we readily promote the need for cooperation, the actual concept of working as a cohesive unit (that is, as a team) implies competition. Constructive competition can have a strong influence on moving people toward developing a "going-places" attitude as well as achieving organizational objectives. However, competition is effective only when combined with an effort to cooperate with others in the organization.

The underlying psychology of competition is based as much on preventing someone or something from getting ahead of us as it is on unifying efforts to achieve a common goal. People compete because to do so fulfills many needs:

- ◆ **Social**—Competition can be used to motivate members of the work group to cooperate and work together as a team.

- ◆ **Security**—Competition can be related to the necessity of at least meeting the achievements of other teams in competitive companies. Doing so is generally accepted as a requirement for the continued growth and prosperity of the organization and its members.

- ◆ **Self-Esteem**—Competition creates an aura of importance related to all tasks, no matter how dull or uninteresting they may seem to be. Thus, the ego of the employee becomes attached to the results achieved.

- ◆ **Achievement**—As a member of a team, individuals gain the opportunity to receive the special recognition and attention associated with being the winner in a competitive situation.

Teams often suffer from complacency because they have been shielded from competition. However, competition should not be confused with controversy or conflict. It is important to understand that a blend of cooperation and competition is necessary to help teams strive to do their best. Generating a constructive competitive spirit that motivates employees to maximize their contributions allows an organization to achieve its goals. Group facilitators can use a variety of games and activities to effectively teach the concept of "cooperative competition."

The inherent structure of games is based on a goal and an accompanying resistance against its achievement. The effort each player makes to overcome the resistance and to achieve the goal is the heart of the activity, central to making it enjoyable and gratifying. In most games, the resistance is supplied by an opponent who is trying to achieve his or her own goal. Your opponent is, therefore, your partner in the game. The best games are those in which you can play your hardest and still count on your opponent to meet your efforts, i.e., to compete with you.

The games presented in this book of activities establish defined physical and/or mental tasks that a team is required to accomplish. Thus, the activities are designed to challenge the physical and mental capabilities of the participants within the team. In most instances, the games require the joint efforts of group members in order to complete the assigned task. The activities are designed to be lessons in determination, teamwork, and planning.

Besides promoting group interaction, the tasks require the participants to work cooperatively on the task at hand, taking advantage of each team member's abilities. In performing the activity, the team must assess and accept the total situation, including the task to be performed and the strengths and limitations of the group as a whole as well as its individual members.

Competitive games can be used for a number of reasons, but most especially to prepare participants for future challenges. These activities take a problem-oriented approach in which the solution is discovered by "doing." Individuals are shown that they can and should become effective group members. Challenging games such as these are a lot of fun, and, at the same time, result in worthwhile learning. A good deal of enjoyable learning experiences can be fostered through these group challenges.

Remember, competition gives training games their vitality. Value should be placed on true competition as well as on the effort made to foster it. As the challenges occur between teams and not between individuals, the opportunity exists for everyone to experience some measure of success. When the activity is debriefed, you should stress the value of the competition but place no extreme importance on the actual winning. The competition should be used as a means for group members to strive to do their best.

Normally, the group will have a number of initial setbacks (due to poor planning, lack of organization, etc.) before successfully completing a task. Therefore, to ensure a successful activity, remember these guidelines: When planning the activity, always try to make the tasks conceivable. In presenting the situation and necessary information, make all rules and procedures clear before the activity begins. Keep the atmosphere light and use humor whenever possible. When a game is prepared in this way, you can step back and give the group the opportunity to devise a plan and to solve the problem, thus creating an environment for learning.

Each activity presented in this book suggests several different content applications. The games can be used to pave the way for the main subject area, or they can become the foundation upon which the desired concepts are built. An activity should be chosen that relates to the main theme or goal of the training session. When selecting an activity, keep in mind the degree of risk taking that is appropriate to the group. It is generally better to err on the conservative side than to run the chance that participants could feel manipulated or vulnerable. This is especially true if the issues are sensitive or controversial. In this way, you will be able to lead the group progressively to new levels of skill, trust, and creativity.

Group size will also affect your choice of games. You will need to match the process to the size of the audience. Suggested discussion areas and procedures are presented for each game, but you should first determine the activity's appropriateness to each group. With a smaller group, you may wish to have every individual report. With a larger group, you may need to limit the discussion to smaller work groups or have one reporter present for each team. As the discussion questions cover a wide range of topics, choose those questions that are appropriate to the topic(s) being addressed.

The time estimated for each game is an approximation and may be adjusted accordingly. Generally, the larger the group, the longer the time required for the activity.

Working Together: 55 Team Games provides group facilitators with exciting and energizing team competitions that help build a constructive competitive spirit for a truly cooperative team effort. As participants discuss their performance in terms of cooperation, leadership, resourcefulness, decision making, efficiency, and initiative, they will develop an awareness of the obligations of each and every member of a group confronted with a challenge.

The general fact is that the most effective way of utilizing human energy is through an organized rivalry, which by specialization and social control is, at the same time, organized cooperation.

Charles Horton Cooley (1864-1929)
U.S. sociologist
Human Nature and the Social Order

1 ◆ Boxing Match

Objective

To encourage teams to strategize and make decisions in a variation of Bingo (placing numbers on a grid that add up to a stated outcome).

Applications

◆ Conflict Resolution

◆ Decision Making

◆ Leadership

◆ Problem Solving

◆ Resource Use

◆ Strategic Planning

Group Size

Unlimited. Participants will work in teams of three to four members each.

Time Required

Ten to twenty minutes.

Materials

Approximately four or five 3" × 5" index cards; a small box to hold all the number cards; a pencil and a Boxing Match Worksheet (customized or the sample provided) for each team; a stopwatch or clock with a second hand (to keep a record of time).

Preparation

Cut the index cards into small squares (one card can make about fifteen small squares). Prepare fifty number cards, five each of the numbers 0 (zero) through 9 (nine). Place the number cards in a small empty box. Copy the Boxing Match Worksheet (one for each team) or create your own customized worksheet using the blank grid provided. If you are creating your own worksheet, print a five-letter word along the top row, placing one letter above each vertical column. Each letter should have a numerical value according to its position in the alphabet (A=1, B=2, etc.) written above it. Each participating team needs one copy of the Boxing Match Worksheet (the original version or the customized version).

Process

1. Instruct the participants to form teams of three to four members each. Have each team select a member to act as its group recorder.

2. Distribute a pencil and one copy of the Boxing Match Worksheet to each participating team. Explain that teams will be playing a game similar to Bingo, but that the object is to make numbers add up to a particular total—the number showing at the top of each column. As a number is called, each team should write that number anywhere on the grid so that all the numbers in a column add up to the total shown at the top. Team members will have a brief period of time to confer each time a number is called before the team recorder adds it to the grid on the Boxing Match Worksheet.

3. Shuffle the numbered cards by shaking the box. Draw one card at a time and call out the number. After calling out the number, place that number card in a separate pile. Allow approximately thirty to sixty seconds for teams to confer on strategy when each number is called. (When the first numbers are called, you may need to allow more time for groups to work together; as play progresses, you can decrease the amount of time for discussion.) The first team to complete a column that adds up correctly is the winner. All numbers used by the winning team must be verified against the cards you have already drawn.

Variations

1. After a designated period of play, each team receives one point for each column completed. The team with the highest number of total points is the winner.

2. Teams may be given a blank grid sheet and allowed to prepare their own game card. The team members print a five-letter word across the top of the grid and randomly assign number values (not to exceed 25) to the letters.

Discussion

♦ What strategy did the team take in planning how to utilize the numbers?

♦ Did this strategy change as the game progressed? Why?

♦ How were decisions reached?

♦ If there were conflicts, how were they resolved?

♦ Who assumed leadership roles?

Boxing Match Worksheet

22	5	9	14	19
V	E	I	N	S

Boxing Match Worksheet -
Customized Version

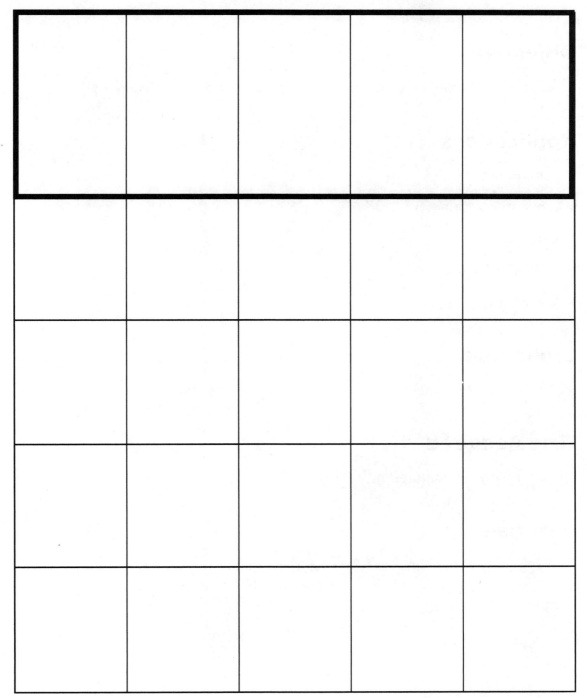

2 ◆ Breaking Away

Objective

To solve a word problem using individual word clues found in balloons.

Applications

◆ Communication

◆ Group Interaction

◆ Icebreaker

◆ Problem Solving

◆ Team Effort

Group Size

Six to thirty participants, who form teams of three members each.

Time Required

Approximately ten minutes.

Materials

Breaking Away paper slips (one for each participant); one balloon for each participant; a large box to hold all the inflated balloons; felt-tip markers in a wide variety of colors.

Preparation

Duplicate the Breaking Away Worksheet (one worksheet provides paper slips for up to thirty participants; use only as many horizontal rows of slips as you need for the total group). Mark each horizontal set of three word clues with one color by drawing a large dot in the top right-hand corner of each (you must use a different color marker for each horizontal set of three slips). Cut the sheets into individual strips following the dashed lines. Prepare one balloon for each participant by placing one rolled paper slip into each balloon before inflating it, and then tying off the end. Place the inflated balloons in a large box or a similar container.

Process

1. Distribute one prepared balloon to each participant. Explain that at your signal the participants will break their balloons to reveal a slip of paper containing a word clue. Players are to locate other players who have a similar color dot marking the slip of paper and to create teams. Team members are to use the words on the slips and rearrange all the letters to spell one long word. All letters must be used and none may be left over. Team members should raise their hands when they have solved the problem.

2. Signal the start of the activity. The facilitator should note the order in which teams finish and announce the winner after all teams have completed the task.

Solution

Every participant needs one pencil and an Alphabet Soup Worksheet.

LACE + PONY + DICE = **ENCYCLOPEDIA**

Discussion

♦ How organized was the overall procedure? Why?

♦ What was the importance of each player to the team's efforts?

♦ What approach did the team take to solve the problem?

♦ How effective was the strategy?

Breaking Away Worksheet

LACE	PONY	DICE
LACE	PONY	DICE
LACE	PONY	DICE
LACE	PONY	DICE
LACE	PONY	DICE
LACE	PONY	DICE
LACE	PONY	DICE
LACE	PONY	DICE
LACE	PONY	DICE
LACE	PONY	DICE

3 ◆ Bridges

Objective

To work in teams constructing a sturdy paper bridge that will withstand weight at the center.

Applications

◆ Creativity

◆ Group Interaction

◆ Problem Solving

◆ Resource Use

Group Size

Eight to thirty participants, who will work in teams of up to five members each.

Time Required

Forty to sixty minutes.

Materials

Newspapers, paper clips, glue, tape, staplers, and scissors; a ruler; a styrofoam cup; one pound of jelly beans; a container (box, pan, or pail).

Preparation

Obtain enough newspapers so that each team will receive five full sheets. The actual amount of paper clips, glue, tape, staplers, and scissors to be provided depends on the number of teams participating; you should limit the supply so that teams are required to share. Place these items on a table that is accessible to all participants.

Process

1. Instruct participants to form teams of up to five members each. Distribute five full sheets of newspaper to each participating team.

2. Explain that the teams will have twenty-five minutes in which to design and construct a bridge from the materials provided. Teams may use as many of the remaining materials as they wish, but supplies are limited and must be shared by all teams. The team with the bridge that can support the most weight will be the winner. The bridges may not be fastened to any structure (e.g., table or chair) and they must span one yard in length.

   The weight (jelly beans in a cup) to test the bridges will be applied to the center of the bridge's span.

3. Signal for the activity to begin. After twenty-five minutes, stop the groups' work and begin to test the bridges. Two members from each team (one at each end) will hold their team's bridge above the ground. The facilitator places the empty styrofoam cup on the center of the bridge span and adds jelly beans until reaching the point where the bridge collapses. (Note: First place a container [box, pan, or pail] under the bridge being tested to catch spillage.) The total number of beans in the cup when a bridge collapses is the weight that it can support. Keep a record of the totals held by each team.

4. Continue testing all the bridges. The bridge that supports the most weight is the winner.

Discussion

♦ How difficult was this task? Why?

♦ What approach did your team take in designing the bridge?

♦ What approach did the team take in constructing the bridge?

♦ How well did team members work together?

♦ How well did teams work together to share the limited resources?

4 ◆ Cable Guide

Objective

To build team trust and cooperation while stringing a cable to connect a span of "islands."

Applications

◆ Communication

◆ Creativity

◆ Group Interaction

◆ Problem Solving

◆ Team Effort

◆ Trust

Group Size

Six to twenty-four participants, who will work in teams of six to eight members each.

Time Required

Twenty to forty-five minutes.

Materials

Rope (4 feet for each team); cable or heavy rope (18 feet for each team); four 2' × 2' cardboard squares for each team.

Preparation

Obtain the following materials *for each participating team*: four cardboard squares (2' × 2'), two 2-foot lengths of rope, one 18-foot length of cable (heavy rope). Position each team at a separate location and allow sufficient space between team work areas. For each team, place the four cardboard squares in a straight line across the floor at equally spaced intervals (approximately four feet apart).

Process

1. Instruct participants to form teams of six to eight members each. Explain that each team must string a cable across a raging river so swift and dangerous that anything that touches it is instantly swept away unless the object is secured in some way.

2. Direct each team to a separately prepared location. Explain that the cardboard squares represent four small islands. The members of the team are to be distributed among these islands, but no inhabitant may be in direct contact with the river (floor). If this happens, the person is immediately swept away from the group.

3. Direct participants to place one of the two short ropes at the first island with the other rope located at the second island; the cable (heavy rope) is at the farthest island. The small ropes are allowed to touch the water (the floor) if someone is holding them. However, if the cable falls into the water (touches the floor), anyone holding it at the time will be swept away into the current. The first team to successfully string the cable without losing any of its members will be the winner of the Nobel Prize in Teamwork!

4. Monitor the activity and lead a discussion when the groups reassemble.

Solution

One of the easiest methods for teams to accomplish the goal is for the second island to throw its rope to the first island. The two ropes are then tied together to make a longer rope that will reach between any two island squares. The cable is then tied to this "new" rope which is thrown to the next island. The group on that island will in turn pull the cable to the island and then pass it on to the next group.

Discussion

♦ How did your team approach the problem?

♦ How difficult was it to coordinate your team's efforts? Why?

♦ What role did communication play in this activity?

♦ How did each member of the team contribute to its overall performance?

♦ Why was trust a determining factor in accomplishing the task?

♦ How does this activity relate to the workplace environment?

5 ◆ Comic Cut-Ups

Objective

To encourage participants to work in teams following prescribed rules to sequence a series of comic strip panels without talking.

Applications

◆ Communication

◆ Group Interaction

◆ Problem Solving

◆ Team Effort

◆ Trust

Group Size

Unlimited. Participants will work in teams of five members each.

Time Required

Twenty to thirty minutes.

Materials

Comic strips (five separate strips containing four cartoon panels each); card stock; colored construction paper; five envelopes for each participating team; one comic strip answer sheet for each team; a clock or timer.

Preparation

Obtain five separate comic strips containing four cartoon panels each. The comics should come from the same feature (e.g., "Peanuts" or "Garfield") but comprise five different versions. Paste the comic strip panels onto a sheet of paper and duplicate one copy on colored stock for each participating team; these will be used as answer sheets. Next, duplicate the comic strip sheet on card stock, one copy per team. Prepare the puzzle pieces by cutting each card stock sheet into twenty separate pieces (i.e., the five comic strips should have a total of twenty comic strip pieces). Keeping each set of twenty pieces together, mix up the pieces and randomly place four strip pieces in each of five envelopes, numbered 1 through 5; each team needs one complete set of envelopes and cards.

Process

1. Instruct participants to form teams of five members each. Distribute a set of five envelopes to each group, giving one envelope to each person.

2. Explain that the purpose of the game is to form five different comic strips, containing four panels each, in proper sequence. During the activity participants are NOT allowed to talk; they must maintain complete silence. Players may give their puzzle piece to another player by handing it to the person they wish to receive it. A player may not point to a piece to indicate that he or she wants it, nor can a player put a piece into another person's puzzle. The object is for each team member to complete a four-panel comic strip, positioned in the appropriate sequence, in front of him or her. Teams will have fifteen minutes to complete the activity.

3. Signal for the activity to begin, and note various group interactions. Indicate when the fifteen-minute time period is up, then distribute one copy of the comic strip answer sheet to each team to review its answers. Lead a group discussion about the game.

Discussion

♦ How well did your team accomplish the task?

♦ How did you as an individual feel about participating in this game?

♦ What were your reactions to not being able to talk?

♦ Did everyone follow the rules? Why?

♦ Did you feel a sense of cooperation and trust within your group? Why or why not?

6 ♦ Commercial Appeal

Objective

To work in groups designing an advertisement depicting your team's strengths.

Applications

♦ Communication

♦ Creativity

♦ Decision Making

♦ Resource Use

♦ Sales

♦ Self-Disclosure

♦ Team Effort

Group Size

Six to forty participants, who will work in teams of up to five members each.

Time Required

Twenty to forty-five minutes.

Materials

One poster board sheet for each team; glue, tape, scissors, a variety of magazines, colored paper, yarn, chalk, colored felt-tip markers, crayons, etc.

Preparation

Obtain poster board sheets, one for each participating team. Place sufficient quantities of the remaining materials on a table that is accessible to all teams.

Process

1. Instruct participants to form teams of up to five members each and distribute one sheet of poster board to each team. Ask the teams to assemble in separate work areas of the room.

2. Explain that each team is to create an advertisement that depicts the combined strengths of its members. In other words, the ad will show those qualities that make the team unique. To accomplish this, the teams should use whatever materials they wish to utilize from the items on the table (indicate where the materials are located).

3. Signal for the activity to begin and allow approximately twenty minutes for group work. Give a five-minute warning before ending the activity.

4. Select one member from each team to comprise a panel of judges that will select the best advertisement.

5. Ask each team to present its advertisement to all the groups, explaining details as necessary. The panel of judges must reach a consensus on which team has the best submission.

Variation

Provide appropriate objects for props (e.g., balls, boxes, books, hats) and have each team produce a skit depicting the team's strengths. Teams then act out their "commercial" in front of everyone; the judges choose the best presentation.

Discussion

♦ What process did the group members use to analyze the team's strengths?

♦ How were these strengths depicted in the advertisements using the supplies provided?

♦ How did the judges reach a decision as to the winning advertisement?

♦ How did individuals feel about being selected to act as a judge?

7 ◆ Common Bonds

Objective

To work creatively in teams solving word connections for a given set of disparate words.

Applications

◆ Communication

◆ Creativity

◆ Goals

◆ Perception

◆ Problem Solving

Group Size

Unlimited. Participants will work in teams of three to four members each.

Time Required

Fifteen to thirty minutes.

Materials

One Common Bonds Worksheet and a pencil for each participant; a flip chart; a felt-tip marker.

Process

1. Direct participants to form teams of three to four members each. Distribute a pencil and one copy of the Common Bonds Worksheet to each group member.

2. Read the instructions at the top of the worksheet and explain that each team will have *approximately* ten minutes to complete the activity. Before beginning, you may wish to provide an example of linking disparate words:

    moon, sun, shoes

    link: "shine"; *added word*: "silver"

3. After allowing enough time for most groups to complete the activity, signal for the activity to end. Review the answers for each group of words, in turn, by writing various team responses on the flip chart. You should first list the link (common bond), then examples of added words. Continue until all responses have been recorded. Suggested connections are listed in the Solutions section below, but any reasonable link should be acceptable.

4. Determine if any team was able to construct its own word set (#11). Record and discuss each example.

Solution

#1 ring	#5 fly	#8 gain
#2 strike	#6 crown	#9 stem
#3 beat	#7 bear	#10 steam
#4 blue		

Discussion

♦ How did this game use both logical and creative thinking?

♦ How does this process apply to problem solving in general? (*You need both types of thinking to get the full picture.*)

♦ Was the "common bond" for each word group easy to identify?

♦ Which ones were more difficult?

♦ What role did perception play in making the connections?

♦ Relate how common goals make a team stronger.

Common Bonds Worksheet

The words in the groups below don't seem to have much in common. Try to think of a common link that binds the words together in some way. Try to think of *at least* one more word to add to each word group. As a bonus, see if you can make your own word group, link, and added word(s) for #11!

#	LINK	WORD GROUP			ADDED WORD
1		tree	telephone	clock	
2		match	bargain	pose	
3		music	policeman	heart	
4		moon	streak	ribbon	
5		bullet	pennant	ball	
6		king	tooth	hat	
7		grudge	burden	witness	
8		wealth	weight	victory	
9		flower	tire	brain	
10		bath	boat	iron	
11					

8 ♦ Crypto-Toon

Objective

To work in teams deciphering and solving the code in a cartoon cryptogram.

Applications

♦ Communication

♦ Group Interaction

♦ Leadership

♦ Problem Solving

♦ Time Pressure

Group Size

Unlimited. Participants will work in teams of three to four members each.

Time Required

Fifteen to twenty minutes.

Materials

A pencil and one Crypto-Toon Handout for each participant; a clock with a second hand or a timer.

Process

1. Instruct participants to form teams of three to four members each. Distribute a pencil and one copy of the Crypto-Toon Handout to each participant.

2. Explain to participants that the cartoon dialogue in the Crypto-Toon Handout has been converted into a cryptogram. In other words, every letter of the alphabet has been consistently replaced by another letter to form a code throughout the entire cartoon.

   To complete the activity, each team is to (1) choose a leader and then (2) find the correct solution for both dialogue "balloons" in the shortest period of time. When a team has finished solving the puzzle, the team leader should stand.

3. Signal for the activity to begin. The facilitator should note the first two teams that complete the task. When the majority of groups has completed the puzzle (or after approximately fifteen minutes have elapsed), signal for the activity to end. At that time, team leaders may be seated. The answers to the Crypto-Toon are revealed by the two winning teams. The first-place team provides the answer to the left-hand balloon; the second-place team provides the answer to the right-hand balloon.

Solution

Left balloon: *How was the stress management workshop you took?*

Right balloon: *Great!* I *worry much more effectively now.*

Discussion

♦ How was the leader chosen on your team?

♦ How did other group members assume task responsibilities?

♦ What methods did the team use to help decipher the code? (*letter patterns, punctuation, etc.*)

♦ How can we relate this process to solving problems that occur on the job?

♦ How does time pressure affect both the quality and quantity of overall team performance?

Crypto-Toon Handout

9 ◆ Degrees of Difference

Objective

To work with group members expressing degrees of difference between two opposite words.

Applications

◆ Change

◆ Communication

◆ Conflict Resolution

◆ Diversity

◆ Problem Solving

◆ Team Effort

Group Size

Five to fifty participants, who will work in teams of five to eight members each.

Time Required

Ten to thirty minutes.

Materials

Cards made from the Degrees of Difference Worksheet; a box to hold the cards; pencils and paper for scoring.

Preparation

Duplicate the Degrees of Difference Worksheet on card stock; cut each sheet into individual word-pair cards following the dashed lines. Place the cards in a box.

Process

1. Instruct participants to form teams of five to eight members each. (The larger the team, the more difficult the task!)

2. Direct the players from each team to form a line. Explain that each team, in turn, will be provided with a word pair that consists of opposite adjectives. Each member of the team will name an item that falls at the extremes and within that range, ordered accordingly. If a player makes a mistake or is unable to name something, the next player must correctly name something for that place.

3. Give the following example for the word pair **cold/hot:** The first player (at one end of the line) names something very cold; the next player names something not quite so cold; the next, something warmer; continuing in increasing degrees until the last player names something very hot. For the cold/hot example, the responses might be: *ice, tap water, milk, coffee, lava, the sun.*

4. Begin the activity by drawing the first card from the box and announcing the word pair to the competing team. Continue drawing new cards until each team has had at least two to three opportunities to play or until all the cards have been played. Keep score for each round; teams receive one point for every correct response. The team with the highest total score at the end of the competition is the winner.

Discussion

♦ How difficult was this task? Why?

♦ How does the process used here relate to the way in which change occurs? (*gradual process that occurs in incremental stages*)

♦ How do varying degrees of difference relate to conflict and its resolution? (*conflict approaches differ with the particular situation; need to look for common ground, conflicting ideas provide new ways to look at things, etc.*)

♦ What role did individual performance play in the overall effort of the team?

♦ How can we relate this game to on-the-job experiences?

Degrees of Difference Worksheet

dull/shiny	hard/soft
short/tall	quiet/loud
wet/dry	sharp/dull
light/heavy	small/large
dark/light	rough/smooth
straight/curved	thick/thin

10 ◆ End of the Line

Objective

To develop team coordination and cooperation while the team moves along a line on stepping stones.

Applications

◆ Change

◆ Communication

◆ Icebreaker

◆ Leadership

◆ Team Effort

Group Size

Five to forty participants, who will work in teams of five members each.

Time Required

Approximately ten minutes.

Materials

Cardboard squares (one for each participant); masking tape.

Preparation

Create one cardboard square for each participant, large enough for a player to stand on it (minimum 1 square foot). Using the masking tape, mark a starting line on the floor for each team of five players, allowing enough space behind the line to accommodate room for the five squares. Mark an ending point approximately ten to fifteen feet from each starting line. (You need a room large enough to provide plenty of space for each team.)

Process

1. Instruct participants to form teams of five members each. Assign each team to a separate starting line and distribute one cardboard square to each participant.

2. Explain that teams are to move in a line from one point to another, utilizing the cardboard squares as stepping stones. Only one player may occupy one square at any time. Team members must coordinate their efforts by relying on the directions of their leader. The last person in line will assume the leadership role for each movement.

3. Give the following directions to the participants:

> Players on each team are to place their squares on the ground in a straight line behind the starting line. Each player is to stand on his or her square. When the facilitator signals for the game to start, the **last** player will say "FORWARD" and each team member will move forward one square. The **first** player will then move to the back of the line, pick up the empty square, return to the front, and place it on the ground. This player will then return to the back and indicate "FORWARD," whereupon all team members will move ahead to occupy a new square. This process is to be repeated until **all** members of a team have crossed their finish line.

4. Signal for the activity to begin. The first team to complete the challenge is the winner.

Discussion

♦ How difficult was it to coordinate the team's efforts?

♦ What role did communication play?

♦ How did you feel about the last person being the leader for the movement?

♦ Why is shared leadership important to teamwork?

11 ◆ Funny Fingers

Objective

To attempt to reach a team goal by transferring balloons from one spot to another in a team relay.

Applications

◆ Group Interaction

◆ Goals

◆ Icebreaker

◆ Team Effort

◆ Time Pressure

Group Size

Eight to thirty participants, who will work in teams of up to ten members each.

Time Required

Approximately ten minutes.

Materials

Construction paper (six 8" × 10" sheets for each team); clear tape and masking tape; a paper towel tube (to mold the "fingers"); round balloons (twelve for each participating team); large cardboard boxes (two for each team) to hold the inflated balloons; a flip chart; a felt-tip marker; a clock or timer.

Preparation

Make "fingers" by rolling a piece of construction paper around the towel tube (not too tightly), taping the seam in several places, and then sliding the paper off the tube. You need to make six "fingers" for each team.

For each team, inflate twelve balloons and place them in a large cardboard box. Using masking tape, mark a starting line on the floor which is approximately twenty feet (eight giant steps) in front of the box holding the balloons. Place a second empty cardboard box approximately twenty feet behind the starting line (in the opposite direction). Repeat this setup for each participating team.

Process

1. Instruct participants to form teams of up to ten members each. The players from each team should form a line behind their team's indicated mark on the floor, facing the box filled with the balloons.

2. Distribute six paper tubes to each group. Explain that each team's challenge will be to use the "fingers" to transport as many balloons as possible in a five-minute period to the end of the line. After the directions are given and before the activity begins, team players on each team will predict how many balloons they will be able to transfer during the allotted time period.

3. Give the following directions to the participants:

> When the signal is given, the first player on the team will put the six tubes on any three fingers of each hand; other team members may help. The player will then leave the starting line, pick up a balloon, bring it back, and place it in the team box at the other end of the line. The "fingers" are to be transferred to the next player in line and the process is repeated until time is called.

Record each team's prediction on a flip chart, then signal for the activity to begin. Give a one-minute warning before time is called.

4. Count the number of balloons in each team's receptacle box and record the actuals next to the predictions on a flip chart. The team that has transferred the most balloons in five minutes is the winner. (If more than one team has trans-

ferred all the balloons, the winner is the team that accomplished the goal in the least amount of time.)

Discussion

♦ How close did your team come in predicting the outcome?

♦ How well did team members work together to coordinate the activity?

♦ What effect did time pressure have on team performance?

♦ What other factors influenced the team's ability to perform the task?

12 ◆ Gizmos

Objective

To share team members' individual knowledge and make team decisions by determining the proper terms for miscellaneous obscure objects.

Applications

◆ Communication

◆ Decision Making

◆ Group Interaction

◆ Leadership

◆ Team Effort

Group Size

Unlimited. Participants will work in teams of up to five members each.

Time Required

Approximately twenty minutes.

Materials

A pencil and a Gizmos Worksheet for each participant; an additional Gizmos Worksheet for each team; a copy of the Gizmos Answer Sheet.

Process

1. Explain that there are some functional objects existing around us which we may not know by their proper terms. This activity will strive to "pool" the group's knowledge to determine the technical terms for certain objects.

2. Distribute a pencil and one copy of the Gizmos Worksheet to each participant. Direct group members to complete the worksheet alone, matching the term they think is correct for each of the ten definitions. Allow approximately five minutes for completion of individual work.

3. When participants have completed the worksheets, instruct them to form teams of up to five members each. Assign one member of each group to act as the team leader.

4. Distribute one copy of the Gizmos Worksheet to each team leader. Explain that group members should work together to come to a *team decision* on the correct answer for each item. The team leader is responsible for coordinating group discussion and recording the team's answers.

5. Allow approximately ten minutes for the group members to work together.

6. Using team feedback and the Gizmos Answer Sheet, review the correct terms for the described items with the participants. You may choose whether or not you wish to provide definitions for the other terms shown on the worksheet (these definitions are provided on the answer sheet).

Discussion

♦ Did group members do better with their individual answers or as a team? Why?

♦ What role did the leader take in the decision-making process?

♦ How does the use of technical terminology and/or acronyms affect the communication process?

♦ What other kinds of "filters" break down communication? (*perception, experience, environment, etc.*)

♦ How can we improve the overall communication process in the workplace?

Gizmos Worksheet

Circle the answer that best matches the definition provided.

1. The small embroidered loop forming a decorative edging on ribbon.

   a) capuche
   b) frizette
   c) picot

2. The metal spike on hiking boots.

   a) crampon
   b) petard
   c) languet

3. The little metal band around a pencil, right below the eraser.

   a) larch
   b) circumflex
   c) ferrule

4. The block or slab on which a statue rests.

   a) foramen
   b) plinth
   c) palanquin

5. The outer rim section of a wheel.

   a) druse
   b) felly
   c) parget

6. The small round pulley that regulates the speed of magnetic tape in a recorder.

   a) capstan
   b) newel
   c) operon

7. The vertical strip dividing the panes of a window.

   a) cullis
   b) filature
   c) mullion

8. The plastic or metal tip of a shoelace.

   a) aglet
   b) gusset
   c) groat

9. The pointed gardening tool that makes holes for planting bulbs.

   a) ostiole
   b) dibble
   c) pawl

10. The small magnifying glass used by jewelers.

    a) lapin
    b) binnacle
    c) loupe

Gizmos Answer Sheet

1. a) Capuche - hood of a cloak
       (esp. the cowl of a Capuchin friar)
    b) Frizette - a curled fringe of hair
    **c) Picot - the small embroidered
    loop forming a decorative edging**

2. **a) Crampon - the metal spike
    on hiking boots**
    b) Petard - a bell-shaped bomb
    c) Languet - thing or part resembling
       tongue in shape or function

3. a) Larch - a coniferous (pine)tree
    b) Circumflex - a phonetic mark
       used over long vowels(Greek)
    **c) Ferrule - the little metal band
    around a pencil, right below the
    eraser, used to strengthen
    the shaft**

4. a) Foramen - medical term
       for a small opening or perforation
    **b) Plinth - the block or slab
    on which a statue rests**
    c) Palanquin - an enclosed litter
       (a conveyance borne on the
       shoulders of men using poles)

5. a) Druse - crystals in a rock cavity
    **b) Felly - the outer rim section
    of a wheel**
    c) Parget - plaster

6. **a) Capstan - the small round pulley
    that regulates the speed of
    magnetic tape in a tape**
    b) Newel - the vertical support on
       a staircase
    c) Operon - a cluster of genes

7. a) Cullis - a gutter
    b) Filature - spinning into thread
    **c) Mullion - the vertical strip
    dividing the panes of a window**

8. **a) Aglet - the plastic or metal
    tip of a shoelace**
    b) Gusset - a triangular garment
       insert
    c) Groat - an old British coin

9. a) Ostiole - a small opening or pore
    **b) Dibble - a pointed gardening
    tool that makes holes for plant-
    ing bulbs**
    c) Pawl - a pivoted device on a
       ratchet wheel

10. a) Lapin - rabbit
    b) Binnacle - a case,box, or stand
       for ship's compass and a lamp
    **c) Loupe - the small magnifying
    glass used by jewelers and
    watchmakers; also used in the
    graphics industry**

13 ◆ Good Fortune

Objective

To work in teams solving a riddle using fortune cookie clues.

Applications

◆ Communication

◆ Icebreaker

◆ Perception

◆ Problem Solving

◆ Team Effort

◆ Time Pressure

Group Size

Four to thirty-six participants, who will work in teams of four members each. (Note: If the total number of participants is not divisible by four—the number of clues in the riddle—you may place the entire riddle on each slip of paper, mark several with a matching number or color to identify each team, and have participants match accordingly.)

Time Required

Approximately ten minutes.

Materials

One clay or Play Doh® "fortune cookie" for every participant.

Preparation

Duplicate the Good Fortune Worksheet. Cut the page into separate slips, keeping each set of four clues together. (The total number of slips possible from one duplicate copy of the worksheet is thirty-six.) To identify the slips in each set, place a matching number on the back of each slip. Number the sets consecutively (1 through 9). (*Note:* See "Group Size" above for a variation to these instructions.)

Press the clay into a thin sheet. Using a crescent-shaped cookie cutter, cut out two crescent shapes for each cookie. Place a rolled paper slip in the center of one crescent and cover it with a second crescent, pressing along the edges to seal. As the clay dries, it will harden to form a "fortune cookie."

Process

1. Distribute one clay "fortune cookie" to each participant. Explain that inside each cookie is a paper slip that reveals one part of a riddle. The players are to locate other players who have a matching number slip and then solve the riddle with this group. Team members should raise their hands when they have the answer. The first team to solve the riddle correctly is the winner.

2. Signal for the game to start. The facilitator should note the order in which teams indicate completion of the game. When all teams are finished, or at the end of five minutes of group work, ask the winning team to reveal the answer. If teams are still unable to determine the answer, you may give the following clue and allow some additional solution time:

    The answer has played a role of burning importance in America since colonial times.

Solution

"TOBACCO"

A cross, a circle complete = T, O

An upright where two semicircles meet = B

A triangle standing on two feet = A

Two semicircles, and a circle complete = C, C, O

Discussion

♦ How difficult was the riddle to solve? Why?

♦ How did your team approach the problem?

♦ How did perception affect communication effectiveness?

♦ Why was each individual so important to the team effort? (*needed all parts of the riddle in order to solve it*)

Good Fortune Worksheet

A cross, a circle complete	*A cross, a circle complete*	*A cross, a circle complete*
An upright where two semicircles meet	*An upright where two semicircles meet*	*An upright where two semicircles meet*
A triangle standing on two feet	*A triangle standing on two feet*	*A triangle standing on two feet*
Two semicircles, and a circle complete	*Two semicircles, and a circle complete*	*Two semicircles, and a circle complete*

A cross, a circle complete	*A cross, a circle complete*	*A cross, a circle complete*
An upright where two semicircles meet	*An upright where two semicircles meet*	*An upright where two semicircles meet*
A triangle standing on two feet	*A triangle standing on two feet*	*A triangle standing on two feet*
Two semicircles, and a circle complete	*Two semicircles, and a circle complete*	*Two semicircles, and a circle complete*

A cross, a circle complete	*A cross, a circle complete*	*A cross, a circle complete*
An upright where two semicircles meet	*An upright where two semicircles meet*	*An upright where two semicircles meet*
A triangle standing on two feet	*A triangle standing on two feet*	*A triangle standing on two feet*
Two semicircles, and a circle complete	*Two semicircles, and a circle complete*	*Two semicircles, and a circle complete*

14 ◆ Headlines

Objective

To work with your team to communicate concepts or messages using newspaper headlines.

Applications

◆ Communication

◆ Content Review

◆ Creativity

◆ Leadership

◆ Perception

Group Size

Unlimited. Participants will work in teams of three or four members each.

Time Required

Twenty to forty-five minutes.

Materials

One felt-tip marker and three copies of the Headlines Worksheet for every team.

Process

1. Instruct the participants to form teams of three to four members each. Distribute a felt-tip marker and three copies of the Headlines Worksheet to each group. Appoint a leader to act as the "editor" for each team.

2. Explain that each team will create a total of three headlines (using the three worksheets) that portray three distinct concepts relating to the group's current training topic. The groups will present their headlines to the reassembled group at the end of the game. *Variation*: You may assign a specific topic to each team (e.g., teamwork, conflict management, communication, technical content, etc.).

3. Signal for the activity to begin and allow ten to fifteen minutes for the groups to work together. Give a five-minute warning before time is called.

4. Reassemble the large group, and instruct the group members of each team to present their three headlines to the rest of the participants and to explain the intent of the message. You may wish to post the Headlines Worksheets in the training room. If you use this game as a pretest of the group's knowledge of the content of the presentation, you may revisit these worksheets at the end of the training session for comparison.

Variations

1. Team members use the back of the Headlines Worksheet to write a short article to accompany each headline.

2. Read an account of some local or national event from a newspaper or magazine. Have team members write an accompanying headline that they will share with the total group. Compare it with the one that was originally published.

Discussion

♦ What kind of role did the "editor" assume during the activity?

♦ How difficult was it to communicate your message? Why?

♦ Did anyone get a different initial perception of headlines presented by other teams? What were they?

♦ How does individual perception affect communication in the workplace?

♦ What specific things can we do to make the communication process more effective?

Headlines Worksheet

EXTRA!! The Times EXTRA!!

15 ◆ Hi-Lo Trivia

Objective

To work in teams analyzing data to determine if the illustrated trivia answer is high or low.

Applications

◆ Data Analysis

◆ Decision Making

◆ Group Interaction

◆ Perception

Group Size

Unlimited. Participants will work in teams of up to five members each.

Time Required

Fifteen to twenty minutes.

Materials

A pencil and one copy each of Hi-Lo Trivia Worksheet 1 and Worksheet 2 for every participant; one copy of the Hi-Lo Trivia Answer Sheet; felt-tipmarkers; a flip chart.

Process

1. Instruct participants to form teams of up to five members each. Distribute a pencil and one copy each of the Hi-Lo Trivia Worksheet 1 and Worksheet 2 to each participant.

2. Explain that this trivia quiz requires the teams to decide if the highlighted number for each statement is too high or too low. Team members should discuss each statement fully and avoid simply guessing. It is not necessary, however, for the team to determine the exact number of the correct answer.

3. Allow approximately ten minutes for the groups to work, giving a two-minute warning before time is called.

4. Use the flip chart to record team answers to each question. Discuss the general trends by looking at how many teams thought an answer was "high" and how many thought it was "low."

5. Using the Hi-Lo Trivia Answer Sheet, provide the correct answers for each item along with additional trivia details. Determine the team with the highest number of correct responses by polling the groups using a show of hands.

Discussion

♦ How did your team arrive at its answers?

♦ What roles did individual team members assume in the decision-making process?

♦ Could you have approached the information differently to increase the likelihood that your answers would have been more accurate? If not, why? If so, how?

♦ How does perception shape our expectations of things?

♦ How does limited background data and perception affect workplace decisions?

Hi-Lo Trivia Worksheet 1

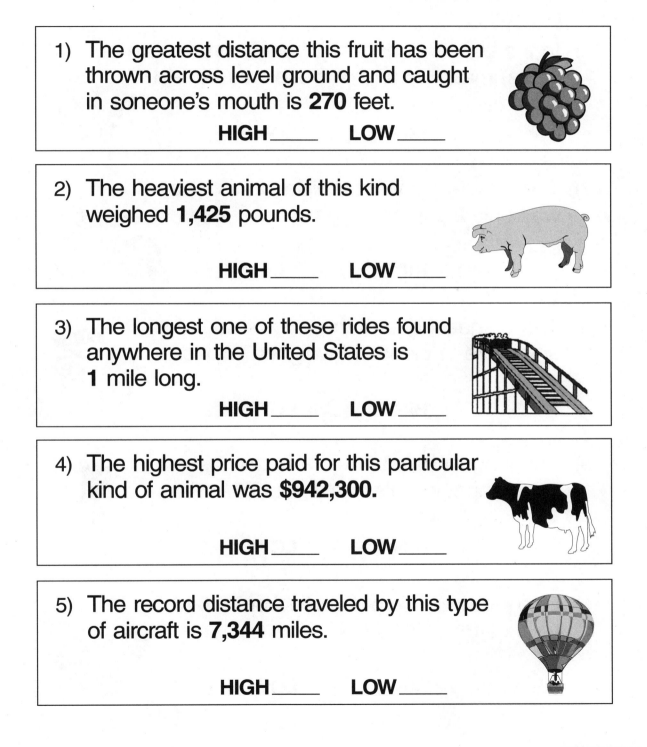

1) The greatest distance this fruit has been thrown across level ground and caught in soneone's mouth is **270** feet.

HIGH_____   LOW_____

2) The heaviest animal of this kind weighed **1,425** pounds.

HIGH_____   LOW_____

3) The longest one of these rides found anywhere in the United States is **1** mile long.

HIGH_____   LOW_____

4) The highest price paid for this particular kind of animal was **$942,300.**

HIGH_____   LOW_____

5) The record distance traveled by this type of aircraft is **7,344** miles.

HIGH_____   LOW_____

Hi-Lo Trivia Worksheet 2

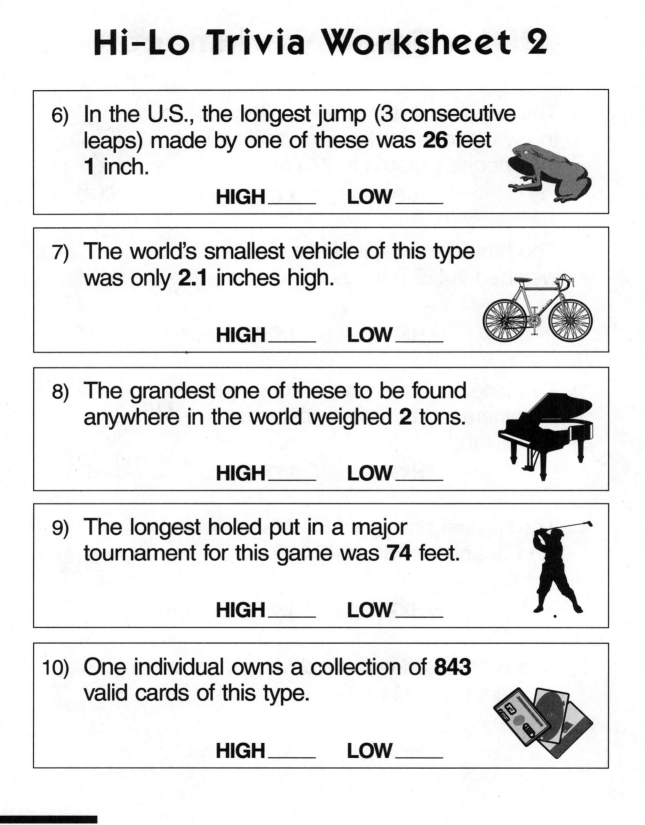

6) In the U.S., the longest jump (3 consecutive leaps) made by one of these was **26** feet **1** inch.

   HIGH_____ **LOW**_____

7) The world's smallest vehicle of this type was only **2.1** inches high.

   HIGH_____ **LOW**_____

8) The grandest one of these to be found anywhere in the world weighed **2** tons.

   HIGH_____ **LOW**_____

9) The longest holed put in a major tournament for this game was **74** feet.

   HIGH_____ **LOW**_____

10) One individual owns a collection of **843** valid cards of this type.

    HIGH_____ **LOW**_____

Hi-Lo Trivia Answer Sheet

1. **Low.** A grape was caught in a person's mouth after a throw of **327.5** feet. James Deady hurled the grape to Paul Tavilla in Boston, Massachusetts, in May 1991.

2. **Low.** The heaviest pig ever recorded weighed **2,552** pounds. "Big Bill" was so fat that his belly dragged on the ground. He was put away after suffering a broken leg in an accident en route to the Chicago World's Fair in 1933.

3. **Low.** The longest roller coaster in the U.S. is **1.4** miles long, including 800 feet of tunnels. "The Beast" is located in Kings Island, near Cincinnati, Ohio.

4. **Low.** The highest price paid for a cow was **$1.3** million. The sale of the Holstein cow occurred in East Montpelier, Vermont, in 1985.

5. **High.** The record distance traveled by a balloon is **5,208.68** miles, by the Raven experimental helium-filled balloon Double Eagle V from November 9-12, 1981. The journey started in Japan and ended in California.

6. **High.** The longest jump (which consists of three consecutive leaps) made by a frog in the U.S. was just under **21½** feet. It was made by an American bullfrog named "Rosie the Ribeter" during the Calaveras Jumping Jubilee on May 18, 1986.

7. **High.** The smallest bicycle in the world had wheels that measured only **0.76** inches. Neville Patten of Gladstone in Queensland, Australia, rode the bike a distance of 13 feet 5½ inches on May 25, 1988.

8. **High.** The largest grand piano ever made weighed **1.4** tons and was 11 feet 8 inches long. It was made in 1935 by Chas H. Challen & Son, Ltd., of London, UK.

9. **Low.** The longest recorded holed putt was **86** feet on the 13th green at the Augusta National (Georgia) by Cary Middlecoff in the 1955 Masters Tournament.

10. **Low.** The largest collection of valid credit cards is **1,356** by Walter Cavanagh of Santa Clara, California. The cards weigh 37½ pounds and are worth more than $1.6 million in credit.

Source: The 1994 Edition of *The Guinness Book of Records*, Bantam Books (New York).

16 ◆ Hunter's Game

Objective

To use only nonverbal actions with other players to hunt for a designated animal while being hunted by other animals.

Applications

◆ Communication

◆ Goals

◆ Icebreaker

◆ Perception

◆ Team Effort

◆ Trust

Group Size

Unlimited. Participants will form teams of six members each.

Time Required

Five to ten minutes.

Materials

Hunter's Game cards.

Preparation

Duplicate the Hunter's Game Worksheet on card stock (one duplicate copy provides a set of game cards for one team of six participants). Cut each set of game cards into separate cards along the dashed lines. *Note:* If the total number of participants is not divisible by six, supplement the game cards with the DECOY cards (the cards at the bottom of the Hunter's Game Worksheet).

Process

1. Distribute one game card to each participant (making sure that players keep their cards concealed from other players). Explain that each of these cards has the name of a particular animal on it that is not to be revealed to other players until later in the activity. Players will participate in a hunt in which each player will hunt for an assigned animal. Without making any sounds, each person must *act out* the animal shown on his or her card while attempting to find the player acting like the animal that the player is assigned to find.

2. Read the following list of animals that shows what animal each player must find. The list is circular:

   ELEPHANT looks for LION

   LION looks for WOLF

   WOLF looks for DOG

   DOG looks for CAT

   CAT looks for MOUSE

   MOUSE looks for ELEPHANT

3. Explain that some participants may have received DECOY cards, in which case the individual may act like any animal to fool the other players. The decoys try to find one another and stay together. Stress that each participant will be both a hunter and a hunted animal. Each team will be comprised of one set of the six animals named or else will contain all DECOYS. When a participant thinks that his or her animal has been found, he or she taps that player on the shoulder; the hunted animal should then show its card to the hunter. If it is the correct animal, the hunter holds on to the player while continuing to search for that

player's prey. In the end, each team should form a circle with the animals holding onto one another.

4. Monitor the activity. When all the teams have formed, lead a discussion with the reassembled group, using the questions below.

Discussion

♦ How difficult was it to find your animal through actions only? Why?

♦ What role does perception play in an activity such as this?

♦ How does nonverbal communication affect the image others have of you?

♦ Why is communication, both verbal and nonverbal, so important in the workplace?

♦ How can we relate this game to teamwork in general? (*players all connected, need for clear communication, common goals, etc.*)

Hunter's Game Worksheet

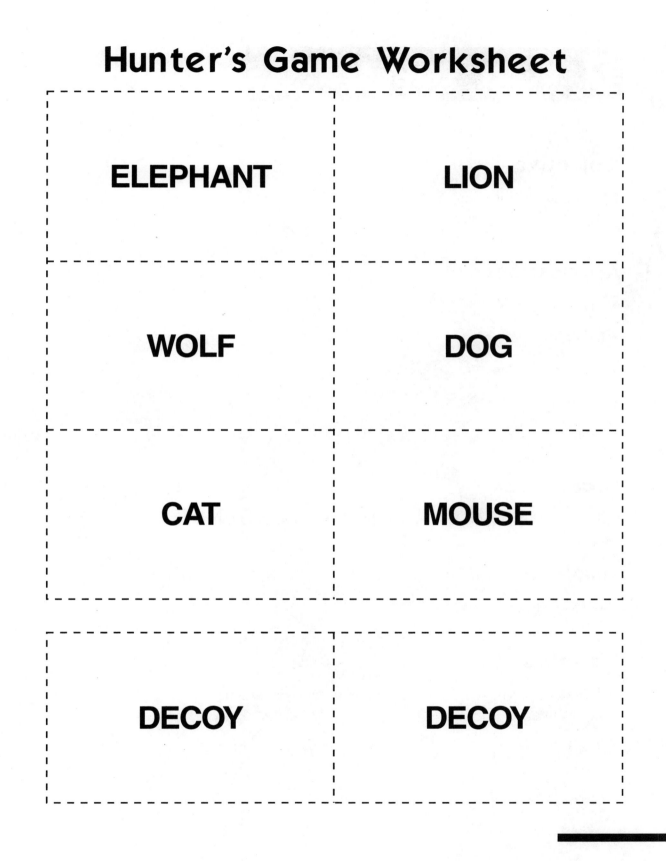

ELEPHANT	**LION**
WOLF	**DOG**
CAT	**MOUSE**
DECOY	**DECOY**

17 ◆ In the Cards

Objective

To compete against other teams by constructing the tallest and most creative tower using playing cards.

Applications

◆ Creativity

◆ Group Interaction

◆ Problem Solving

◆ Strategic Planning

◆ Team Effort

Group Size

Unlimited. Participants will work in teams of three to four members each.

Time Required

Twenty-five to forty minutes.

Materials

One deck of playing cards for each team; a ruler or yardstick; a clock with a second hand or timer.

Process

1. Instruct participants to form teams of three to four members each. Distribute one deck of playing cards to each participating team.

2. Explain that each team's challenge is to construct a card tower, using an entire deck of cards, within a twenty-minute time period. No other materials except the playing cards may be used. If a tower collapses, the team working on it may start over again, but the clock keeps ticking. At the end of the twenty-minute time limit, the towers will be judged for both height and creativity. In the first category, the tallest tower standing long enough to be measured is the winner. In the second category, everyone votes to determine the most creatively designed tower.

3. Signal for the activity to begin and monitor progress. Give a five-minute warning before the twenty-minute time period is over.

4. Determine the tallest tower of cards and announce the winning team in the height category. Then have participants vote to determine the most creatively designed tower and announce the winner in the second category.

Discussion

♦ How did you feel about participating in this activity?

♦ How well did group members work together as a team? Why?

♦ How many of the total cards were you able to use to construct your tower?

♦ What approach did the team take toward fulfilling this challenge?

♦ What factors did you need to consider in planning the structure?

♦ Did you need to make adjustments as you proceeded? If so, what kind?

♦ How does this activity relate to projects undertaken in the workplace?

18 ◆ Key to the City

Objective

To use limited methods of communication to identify an assigned city.

Applications

◆ Communication

◆ Data Analysis

◆ Icebreaker

◆ Problem Solving

◆ Team Effort

◆ Trust

Group Size

Unlimited.

Time Required

Fifteen to thirty minutes.

Materials

One city identification card for each participating player (see instructions below); a felt-tip marker; a hole puncher; scissors; one sheet of construction paper and two feet of yarn for each participant.

Preparation

Make city identification cards from construction paper, writing the name of a different city in large letters on each card. The cities may be restricted to the United States or be from anywhere in the world. Some examples include New York, New Orleans, Los Angeles, London, Paris, and Cairo. Each participant needs to receive a different city identification card. The sheets should be punched with two holes, at opposite upper corners, and a string of about two feet of yarn should be placed through the holes and tied in a loop.

Process

1. Explain that each participant will be assigned the secret identity of a city. To uncover their own identities, participants are to move around the room and seek help from the other group members. They may ask each person up to three questions that can be answered only with a "YES," "NO," or "I DON'T KNOW" response. Remind respondents that they must limit their answers to these three reply choices. Once players discover what city they are, they are to move the card they are wearing around and wear the identity on their chest. They should continue to circulate with other players, giving hints to those who have not yet discovered what city they are.

2. Distribute one city identification card, face down, to each participant. Instruct players *not* to turn their cards over or reveal the identity of their card to other players. At your signal, each person is to turn to another participant and place the sheet around that individual's neck so that the name of the city appears on the player's back and the city is not revealed to the player wearing the card.

3. After everyone has put on the city cards, signal for the activity to begin. Allow sufficient time for group interaction. You may wish to set a specific time limit at the beginning of the activity, or stop the group when at least a majority of cities has been identified.

Discussion

♦ What types of questions did you ask?

♦ How helpful were the responses you received?

♦ What impact did the restricted answers have on solving the problem?

♦ Were some cities easier to identify than others? Why? (*familiarity with place through experience, knowledge, etc.*)

♦ How did you feel about the need to rely on information given to you by the other players?

♦ Relate this game to problem solving and teamwork in the workplace.

19 ◆ Knot Now

Objective

To straighten out a tangled knot of team members.

Applications

◆ Communication

◆ Icebreaker

◆ Group Interaction

◆ Leadership

◆ Problem Solving

Group Size

Eight to forty participants, who will work in teams of eight to ten members each.

Time Required

Ten to twenty minutes.

Materials

None.

Process

1. Request that participants form teams of eight to ten members each. Explain that each team's challenge will be to create a tangled knot of hands and then to untangle the knot.

2. Separate each team in a different location or section of the training area and have the members of each group form a circle.

3. After each team forms a circle, each team player should reach across with his or her right hand and hold someone else's right hand. Next, each member reaches across with the left hand and finds someone else to hold his or her left hand. A tangled knot is formed.

4. Once each team forms a tangled knot, the facilitator should create one break in the knot of each group; the two people at the break will let go of their hands at the break, but will continue holding with their other hands. Then the two "loose ends," now the team leaders, will attempt to form the circled maze of hands into a straight line. Everyone in the team other than the two leaders must remain intact.

Variations

1. Team members form a circle, place their hands in the center, and take hold of the hands of two people other than those immediately next to them. The group then works together in an attempt to untie the knot without releasing hand-holds.

2. Two players stay separate from the group, with their backs turned. The rest of the participants hold hands in a circle and twist themselves over and under and through one another without dropping hands. The two extra players then try to untangle the group.

Discussion

♦ How did the players who were designated as leaders to untangle the group feel about the game?

♦ What process was used to untangle the group?

♦ Was this process effective?

♦ How well were directions communicated within the team?

20 ◆ Line-Up

Objective

To work cooperatively with other team players in a race to form a sequential line that represents announced numbers.

Applications

- ◆ Communication
- ◆ Content Review
- ◆ Data Analysis
- ◆ Group Interaction
- ◆ Icebreaker
- ◆ Team Effort

Group Size

Twelve to fifty participants, who will work in equal-size teams of up to ten members each. (You need a minimum of two teams for this game.)

Time Required

Approximately ten minutes.

Materials

Paper or card stock (one sheet per player); one set of numbered cards for each team; a felt-tip marker; a flip chart.

Preparation

Determine the number of players participating and the number of teams that will be formed during the activity (each team should have an equal number of participants; the maximum number of players on a team is ten). You need to prepare a set of numbered cards for each team, one card per player, by writing one number on each card according to the following rule:

> If you have ten players on each team, you will use the numbers 0 through 9 for each set of cards; for seven players on each team, use the numbers 0 through 6 for each set; etc. *Note*: Keep each set of numbered cards together for distribution to the teams.

Also determine a series of ten or more numbers that you will call out during the game using the numbers on the cards (e.g., if you have teams of ten players each, you use cards numbered 0 through 9; possible number combinations are 932, 4502, 78153, 67). *Note*: Use only those numbers included in the card sets provided (e.g., exclude numbers 8 and 9 if team cards are numbered from 0 to 7 for groups of eight members). You are also restricted to using a particular number card once each time you call out a number; in other words, you cannot use the number "544" because there is only one card 4 available in each group.

Process

1. Divide the group of participants into equal teams. Separate each team in a different area of the training room, and have group members stand together. Provide one set of numbered cards to each group so that every player receives one card.

2. Explain that a number will be announced by the facilitator, such as "126." The players on each team who are holding the cards that comprise this number (1, 2, and 6) are to form a line in the appropriate sequence (showing their numbered cards). The first team to line up correctly for the number announced will receive one point. The first team to accumulate 10 points wins the game.

3. Signal for the activity to begin and keep score on the flip chart.

Variations

1. Call out mathematical problems that require addition, subtraction, multiplication, or division to produce the number to be formed. For example, you may say, "Add 2, 8, and 7 then subtract 3" so players will determine the answer, which is "14" (players with cards 1 and 4 line up to show the answer 14).

2. When teaching a technical class that requires information involving numbers, use questions or problems relating to specific data.

3. Print letters of the alphabet on the cards and announce words that teams will form. Be sure to use only those words that correspond to the letters provided— and no double-letter words!

Discussion

♦ What, if anything, made this game difficult?

♦ What was the importance of each individual player to the team's overall performance?

♦ How can we relate this game to the use of specific team roles in the workplace?

21 ◆ Locomotion

Objective

To traverse a course as a team without breaking the connection.

Applications

◆ Communication

◆ Goals

◆ Group Interaction

◆ Leadership

◆ Team Effort

Group Size

Twelve to forty participants, who will form teams of six to eight members each.

Time Required

Ten to thirty minutes.

Materials

A box of spaghetti noodles (at least 150 unbroken noodles); enough string or yarn to run a trail throughout the training room; a stopwatch or a watch with a second hand; a flip chart (optional).

Preparation

Make a trail by running string or yarn throughout the room for the teams to follow. You should design a course that is sufficiently challenging without presenting dangerous or frustrating maneuvers.

Process

1. Instruct the participants to form teams of six to eight members each. Select one member from each group to act as a team leader.

2. Explain that each team will move as quickly as possible throughout the course that has been designed in the training room. During the game, it is important for each team to "stick together"; in order to do this, players will hold a raw spaghetti noodle between each team member. Players must not let go of the noodles or break them. The entire team must STOP if a noodle breaks. The leader, who should be located at the head of the team, will have twenty extra noodles to replace any broken ones. However, one penalty point is assigned for each piece of broken spaghetti. The leader will be responsible for leaving his or her place in line to replace any broken noodles. The group may proceed on the course only when the leader has returned to the head of the team. Only one team will be allowed on the course at a time. The team that maneuvers through the trail in the least amount of time combined with the lowest number of penalty points is the winner.

3. As each team prepares to traverse the course, hand a spaghetti noodle to each team member to hold as a connection to the person ahead of him or her. In addition, provide the leader with twenty extra noodles to replace broken ones during the activity. Time each team as it walks the course. Record the elapsed time and assign any penalty points for replacing broken noodles. Follow this procedure for each participating team.

Discussion

♦ How did individual team members feel during this game?

♦ How did the assigned role of the leader affect team performance?

♦ If a noodle broke, how was the leader informed?

♦ Did group members feel that the team performed as well as they thought it would? Why?

♦ What changes could have been made to improve the team's overall performance?

♦ In what way does group size affect teamwork in general?

22 ♦ Losing Your Marbles

Objective

To deal with probability by predicting the color combinations of marbles drawn from another team's hidden set of marbles.

Applications

♦ Data Analysis

♦ Change

♦ Decision Making

♦ Problem Solving

♦ Risk Taking

♦ Trust

Group Size

Six to thirty participants, who will work in teams of up to five members each. (You need a minimum of two teams for this game.)

Time Required

Ten to thirty minutes.

Materials

Ten to twelve marbles (beads or checkers) in two different colors for each team; an empty box or container to hold all the marbles; a paper bag, a blank sheet of paper, and a pencil for each team.

Preparation

Place approximately ten to twelve marbles (beads or checkers) times the number of teams in an empty box or container.

Process

1. Instruct participants to form teams of up to five members each (the minimum number of teams required is two). Explain that teams will compete against each other in sets of two (or three) teams.

2. Distribute a blank sheet of paper, a pencil, and a paper bag to each participating team.

   Explain that teams will predict the selection of marble sets from their opponents based on preliminary data. The resulting information may change as acquisitions occur, and each team will be given a brief period of time between plays to discuss decisions. Teams may use the paper and pencils to take notes during play.

3. One at a time, have each team choose eight marbles, in any color combination, from the large container. Each team will place the selected marbles in its own paper bag. One team will then tell the other competing team the number and color of the marbles in its bag; for example, "five red and three black." One team will be selected from each competing set of two to three groups to start the activity. Explain that each team, in turn, is to draw two marbles at a time from the other team's bag, but first it must predict the colors that will be drawn. Teams members may discuss their strategy before proceeding with the next play. If a guess is wrong, the marbles are returned to the opposing team's bag. If the guess is correct, the guessing team keeps the marbles it drew and adds them to its own bag. Explain that a team must win all the other team's marbles in order to win the game, or the facilitator may determine a set time of play with the winning team being the one that possesses the most marbles at the end of the allotted time.

4. Signal for the activity to begin. Stop play at the predetermined time or when the first team acquires all of its opponent's marbles. Announce the winning team.

Discussion

This game deals with probability: the understanding of chance, greater or lesser likelihood, necessity, impossibility and equal odds.

♦ How did teams decide what predictions to make?

♦ How can we use this type of information (probability) in judging what risks to take?

♦ What effect did the changing composition of marbles have on your decision-making strategy?

♦ How can we relate this to change that occurs in the workplace? (*conditions change, flexibility needed, review of current situations in terms of past, etc.*)

23 ◆ May the Fourth Be With You

Objective

To reach consensus on the fourth-ranked item in a series of questionnaire responses.

Applications

◆ Conflict Resolution

◆ Data Analysis

◆ Decision Making

◆ Group Interaction

◆ Leadership

Group Size

Unlimited. Participants will work in teams of four members each.

Time Required

Twenty to forty minutes.

Materials

A pencil and one copy each of the May the Fourth Be With You Worksheets 1 and 2 for each participant; a May the Fourth Be With You Answer Sheet; a clock or timer.

Process

1. Instruct participants to form teams of four members each. Ask each team to select one member to act as its team recorder.

2. Distribute a pencil and one copy each of the May the Fourth Be With You Worksheets 1 and 2 to each participant. Explain that the worksheets contain a variety of topics to test the decision-making skills of the team. The series of responses provided for each question represent the top five answers to the topic described. Team members are instructed to work together to select *only* the **fourth-ranked item** in that series. The recorder for each team is responsible for circling the team answer.

3. Allow sufficient time for the groups to work together openly discussing the items and completing the worksheets. When the teams have finished, review the answers using the Answer Sheet provided. The answers presented show all five items in proper sequence. By a show of hands, determine which team has the most correct answers to determine the winning team(s).

Discussion

♦ Did the team's recorder assume the leadership role? Why?

♦ How did the team make its decisions?

♦ Did the decision-making process remain the same for all questions? Why?

♦ Did any conflicts emerge during the game? How were they resolved?

May the Fourth Be With You
Worksheet 1

1. **4th Largest City**

   Mexico City, Mexico
   New York, United States
   Sao Paulo, Brazil
   Tokyo-Yokohama, Japan
   Seoul, South Korea

2. **4th Largest Ocean**

   Atlantic Ocean
   Indian Ocean
   Arctic Ocean
   Mediterranean Sea
   Pacific Ocean

3. **4th Largest River**

   Amazon
   Nile
   Yangtze Kiang
   Ob
   Mississippi-Missouri-
     Red Rock

4. **4th Largest Island**

   Borneo
   New Guinea
   Baffin
   Greenland
   Madagascar

5. **4th Largest National Park
   in the "Lower 48"**

   Everglades
   Yellowstone
   Olympic
   Glacier
   Grand Canyon

6. **4th State to Ratify the
   Constitution**

   Pennsylvania
   Delaware
   Connecticut
   New Jersey
   Georgia

7. **4th U.S. Vice President**

   Thomas Jefferson
   Elbridge Gerry
   George Clinton
   Aaron Burr
   John Adams

8. **4th in Line of Presidential
   Succession**

   Secretary of the Treasury
   Speaker of the House
   President Pro Tempore of Senate
   Vice President
   Secretary of State

9. **4th State to Secede From
   the Union**

   Florida
   South Carolina
   Georgia
   Alabama
   Mississippi

10. **4th Person in Space**

    Alan B. Shepard, Jr.
    John H. Glenn, Jr.
    L. Gordon Cooper, Jr.
    Gherman S. Titov
    Yuri A. Gagarin

May the Fourth Be With You
Worksheet 2

11. 4th Highest Magazine Circulation

Better Homes & Gardens
TV Guide
Reader's Digest
Good Housekeeping
National Geographic

12. 4th Tallest Building in the U.S. (# stories)

World Trade Center (New York)
Sears Tower (Chicago)
Amoco (Chicago)
Empire State (New York)
John Hancock (Chicago)

13. 4th Longest U.S. Automobile Tunnel

Fort McHenry (Baltimore)
Lincoln (New York)
Brooklyn-Battery (New York)
Holland (New York)
Hampton Roads (Norfolk)

14. 4th President of the United States

George Washington
James Madison
James Monroe
Thomas Jefferson
John Adams

15. 4th Book of the Old Testament

Exodus
Deuteronomy
Genesis
Numbers
Leviticus

16. 4th Planet From the Sun

Mercury
Jupiter
Venus
Earth
Mars

17. 4th Winner of the Super Bowl (Super IV)

Baltimore Colts
Dallas Cowboys
Green Bay Packers
New York Jets
Kansas City Chiefs

18. 4th Leading Home-Run Hitter

Babe Ruth
Hank Aaron
Harmon Killebrew
Willie Mays
Frank Robinson

19. 4th Most Populous U.S. State (1990 Census)

California
Florida
New York
Pennsylvania
Texas

20. 4th Most Populous Age Group in U.S. (1993 Census)

Under 5
25-29
30-34
35-39
40-44

May the Fourth Be With You
Answer Sheet 1

1. **4th Largest City**

   Mexico City, Mexico
   New York, United States
   Sao Paulo, Brazil
   Tokyo-Yokohama, Japan
   *Seoul, South Korea

2. **4th Largest Ocean**

   Atlantic Ocean
   Indian Ocean
   *Arctic Ocean
   Mediterranean Sea
   Pacific Ocean

3. **4th Largest River**

   Amazon
   Nile
   *Yangtze Kiang
   Ob
   Mississippi-Missouri-Red Rock

4. **4th Largest Island**

   Borneo
   New Guinea
   Baffin
   Greenland
   *Madagascar

5. **4th Largest National Park in the "Lower 48"**

   Everglades
   Yellowstone
   Olympic
   *Glacier
   Grand Canyon

6. **4th State to Ratify the Constitution**

   Pennsylvania
   Delaware
   Connecticut
   New Jersey
   *Georgia

7. **4th U.S. Vice President**

   Thomas Jefferson
   Elbridge Gerry
   *George Clinton
   Aaron Burr
   John Adams

8. **4th in Line of Presidential Succession**

   Secretary of the Treasury
   Speaker of the House
   President Pro Tempore of Senate
   Vice President
   *Secretary of State

9. **4th State to Secede from the Union**

   Florida
   South Carolina
   Georgia
   *Alabama
   Mississippi

10. **4th Person in Space**

    Alan B. Shepard, Jr.
    *John H. Glenn, Jr.
    L. Gordon Cooper, Jr.
    Gherman S. Titov
    Yuri A. Gagarin

May the Fourth Be With You
Answer Sheet 2

11. **4th Highest Magazine Circulation**

    *_Better Homes & Gardens_
    TV Guide
    Reader's Digest
    Good Housekeeping
    National Geographic

12. **4th Tallest Building in the U.S. (# stories)**

    World Trade Center (New York)
    Sears Tower (Chicago)
    Amoco (Chicago)
    Empire State (New York)
    *John Hancock (Chicago)

13. **4th Longest U.S. Automobile Tunnel**

    *Fort McHenry (Baltimore)
    Lincoln (New York)
    Brooklyn-Battery (New York)
    Holland (New York)
    Hampton Roads (Norfolk)

14. **4th President of the United States**

    George Washington
    *James Madison
    James Monroe
    Thomas Jefferson
    John Adams

15. **4th Book of the Old Testament**

    Exodus
    Deuteronomy
    Genesis
    *Numbers
    Leviticus

16. **4th Planet from the Sun**

    Mercury
    Jupiter
    Venus
    Earth
    *Mars

17. **4th Winner of the Super Bowl (Super Bowl IV)**

    Baltimore Colts
    Dallas Cowboys
    Green Bay Packers
    New York Jets
    *Kansas City Chiefs

18. **4th Leading Home-Run Hitter**

    Babe Ruth
    Hank Aaron
    Harmon Killebrew
    Willie Mays
    *Frank Robinson

19. **4th Most Populous U.S. State (1990 Census)**

    California
    *Florida
    New York
    Pennsylvania
    Texas

20. **4th Most Populous Age Group in U.S. (1993 Census)**

    Under 5
    *25-29
    30-34
    35-39
    40-44

24 ◆ Minor 49er

Objective

To determine the costs and number of work hours required to pay for a date in 1949.

Applications

◆ Conflict Resolution

◆ Data Analysis

◆ Decision Making

◆ Group Interaction

◆ Problem Solving

Group Size

Unlimited. Participants will work in teams of up to five members each.

Time Required

Thirty to forty-five minutes.

Materials

A pencil and one copy each of the Minor 49er Scenario Handout and the Minor 49er Worksheet for each participant; the Minor 49er Solution Sheet; a flip chart; a felt-tip marker.

Preparation

Prepare a sheet of flip-chart newsprint with the following information:

RULES FOR CONSENSUS

(1) No voting.

(2) Commitment to idea.

(3) Express views fully.

(4) Desire to meet group needs.

Process

1. Instruct participants to form teams of up to five members each. Distribute a pencil and one copy each of the Minor 49er Scenario Handout and the Minor 49er Worksheet to each participant.

2. Explain that group members are to work together to solve the problem. The teams should reach a consensus on the worksheet choices; a full discussion of the information is necessary. Refer to the prepared flip-chart sheet, reviewing the Rules for Consensus with the groups.

3. Read aloud the Minor 49er Scenario Handout, then direct participants to the instructions on the Minor 49er Worksheet. Stress that the final solution should be rounded to the nearest two decimal places. Tell the teams that they will have approximately twenty minutes to complete the activity.

4. Signal for the activity to begin. Give a five-minute warning before the time expires.

5. Using a blank sheet of flip-chart newsprint, record each team's solution to the required work hours. Review the answer to each item according to the information provided on the Minor 49er Solution Sheet. Reveal the final solution and explain how it was calculated.

6. Compare the final solution of 25.00 hours to the groups' answers recorded on the flip chart. The winning team is the one that comes closest to the correct number of work hours required to pay for the date.

Discussion

♦ How close did your team come to determining the actual answer?

♦ What factors influence the use of data?

♦ How does this relate to problem solving in general?

♦ In what situations would consensus decision making be most effective?

♦ How were team roles and responsibilities determined?

♦ How were conflicts resolved?

♦ How does group size affect team performance?

Minor 49er Scenario Handout

It was April 1949 and 17-year-old Tommy Smith had just made a date with Mary Lou Butler for the following Saturday night! Mary Lou was the girl he had been dreaming about all year. If he was lucky and things went well, she might even go to the prom with him the next month. Tommy wanted everything to be perfect, so he began making his plans.

First, they would go to the cinema to see Broderick Crawford in *All the King's Men.* (The newspaper had said that it was a sure winner for the Academy Awards that year.) After the movie, he and Mary Lou would stop for a Coke® at the malt shop. Finally, Tommy would bring her back to his house to listen to some music before he had to drive her home.

Tommy hoped his Dad would let him use the Plymouth the next weekend. Since Dad usually filled the tank with gas every Saturday, Tommy would offer to pay for the full 10 gallons if only he could have the car for the whole evening.

Tommy wanted to look his best, of course, so he would need to stop at the drugstore on Saturday morning for a bottle of Vitalis hair tonic, a new razor, and blades. He could even drop in to the Midway Music Shop on the way and get that new Sinatra record he had been planning to buy. (Mary Lou had commented on how much she liked the songs.)

The question now was, "How many hours did Tommy need to work bagging at the grocery store to cover all his expenses?" Minimum wages don't go very far!!

Minor 49er Worksheet

ITEM	1949 COST	TOTAL
Bottle of Vitalis	a) .25¢ b) .55¢ c) .80¢	
Razor and 10 blades	a) $1.00 b) $1.35 c) $1.75	
12" LP record	a) $3.30 b) $4.15 c) $4.85	
Gallon of gasoline	a) .19¢ b) .26¢ c) .30¢	
Movie admission	a) .45¢ b) .60¢ c) .80¢	
Glass of Coke®	a) .05¢ b) .10¢ c) .20¢	

TOTAL COST

1949 Minimum Wage:　　　a) .40¢/hr.
　　　　　　　　　　　　b) .55¢/hr.
　　　　　　　　　　　　c) .65¢/hr.

NUMBER OF REQUIRED WORK HOURS: _____

Minor 49er Solution Sheet

ITEM	1949 COST	TOTAL
Bottle of Vitalis	a) .25¢	a) .25¢
Razor and 10 blades	a) $1.00	a) $1.00
12" LP record	c) $4.85	c) $4.85
Gallon of gasoline	b) .26¢	c) $2.60
Movie admission	b) .60¢ x 2 people	c) $1.20
Glass of Coke®	a) .05¢ x 2 people	c) .10¢
TOTAL COST		**$10.00**

1949 Minimum Wage: a) .40¢/hr.

NUMBER OF REQUIRED WORK HOURS: 25.00

Total Cost ($10.00) ÷ Minimum Wage ($.40/hr) = 25.00

25 ♦ Number Express

Objective

To solve a numerical equation puzzle to reveal the key number.

Applications

♦ Data Analysis

♦ Decision Making

♦ Group Interaction

♦ Problem Solving

♦ Time Pressure

Group Size

Unlimited. Participants will work in teams of three to four members each.

Time Required

Five to ten minutes.

Materials

A pencil and a copy of the Number Express Puzzle Worksheet for each participant; a Number Express Solution Sheet.

Process

1. Instruct participants to form teams of three to four members each. Distribute a pencil and a copy of the Number Express Puzzle Worksheet to each participant.

2. Explain that each clue in the puzzle is presented in the form of a two-part equation. The team as a whole should discern the answers to both parts, perform the calculation indicated, and write the result in the box corresponding to the letter of the clue. After all the boxes have been correctly filled in, each horizontal and vertical line will total a key number.

3. Signal for the activity to begin. When a team completes the entire puzzle (filling all the squares and determining the key number), all group members should stand. The facilitator should note the order in which teams finish. When all teams have finished, have everyone be seated.

4. Review the answer to each block using participant feedback and referring to the Number Express Solution Sheet.

Discussion

♦ How was the task approached by the team?

♦ How well did team members work together?

♦ What significance did working with numbers have on the task as a whole?

♦ Were any special problems encountered? If so, what kind?

♦ How were these problems resolved?

♦ How did pressure to complete the task quickly affect overall team performance?

Number Express Puzzle

A	F	K	P	U
B	G	L	Q	V
C	H	M	R	W
D	I	N	S	X
E	J	O	T	Y

KEY NUMBER = _____

A) Ounces in lb. - "Uno"
B) Fourscore ÷ Quarters in dollar
C) RPM of a "single" ÷ _____Ring Circus
D) Number of winks in a nap - Olympic Rings
E) Dalmations - Piano Keys
F) One gross ÷ Inches in ft.
G) Supreme Court members x Seasons in year
H) Lives of a cat x Pair
I) Deadly Sins x Sides on square
J) Piano Keys ÷ "Catch_____"
K) Strikes in an out + Apostles
L) _____Mile Island x Days in a week
M) Ali Baba's Thieves - Bakers Dozen
N) "Blackjack" - Trivial Pursuit categories
O) "Calling Birds" x Points on a star
P) Sawbuck + Quarts in gallon
Q) Minutes in hour ÷ "Little Indians"
R) Decade + Months in year
S) Octopus legs + "Commandments"
T) Days in April + Legs on Spider
U) Feet in fathom x Days in week
V) Months in year + _____ Stooges
W) Route _____ - U.S. states
X) Alphabet letters ÷ Original U.S. colonies
Y) Days in fortnight + Tic-Tac-Toe squares

Number Express Solution Sheet

A	**15**	F	**12**	K	**15**	P	**14**	U	**42**
B	**20**	G	**36**	L	**21**	Q	**6**	V	**15**
C	**15**	H	**18**	M	**27**	R	**22**	W	**16**
D	**35**	I	**28**	N	**15**	S	**18**	X	**2**
E	**13**	J	**4**	O	**20**	T	**38**	Y	**23**

KEY NUMBER = 98

A) 16 - 1
B) 80 ÷ 4
C) 45 ÷ 3
D) 40 - 5
E) 101 - 88
F) 144 ÷ 12
G) 9 x 4
H) 9 x 2
I) 7 x 4
J) 88 ÷ 22
K) 3 + 12
L) 3 x 7
M) 40 - 13

N) 21 - 6
O) 4 x 5
P) 10 + 4
Q) 60 ÷ 10
R) 10 + 12
S) 8 + 10
T) 30 + 8
U) 6 x 7
V) 12 + 3
W) 66 - 50
X) 26 ÷ 13
Y) 14 + 9

26 ◆ Objectivity

Objective

To work in teams brainstorming ways in which to use a commonplace object.

Applications

◆ Creativity

◆ Group Interaction

◆ Icebreaker

◆ Team Effort

Group Size

Unlimited. Participants will work in teams of up to six members each.

Time Required

Five to ten minutes.

Materials

A familiar object (e.g., a ruler, styrofoam cup, belt, box); a pencil and a copy of the Objectivity Worksheet for each participating team; a flip chart; a felt-tipmarker; a clock with a minute hand or a timer.

Preparation

Obtain a familiar object to display. If you are unable to locate the actual object, you may wish to have a picture of it or merely describe the object to the teams.

Duplicate one copy of the Objectivity Worksheet for each participating team. (If possible, place a small picture of the designated object on the master sheet prior to duplication.)

Process

1. Instruct participants to form teams of up to six members each. Distribute a pencil and a copy of the Objectivity Worksheet to each team. Each team should select a team leader who will record the group's work.

2. Explain that each team is to brainstorm a list of ways in which a common object can be used. The team with the *longest* list of *workable* uses at the end of five minutes will be the winner.

3. Display the object (or describe it) and signal for the activity to begin.

4. Stop the activity after five minutes. Determine the team with the highest number of uses for the object. Using participant feedback, make a composite list of all possible ideas and post them on a flip chart. Count the total number of suggestions on the composite list and compare it with the highest team score.

Discussion

♦ Were there suggestions made by others that you had not considered?

♦ How does this game relate to teamwork in general?

♦ How can we equate this game to brainstorming as a tool for decision making?

Objectivity Worksheet

OBJECT: _____

TOTAL NUMBER OF IDEAS GENERATED: _____

27◆ Pinned

Objective

To attempt to position your team's ball as close to the target as possible without knocking it down.

Applications

◆ Change

◆ Goals

◆ Leadership

◆ Problem Solving

◆ Strategic Planning

◆ Team Effort

Group Size

Five to thirty participants, who will work in teams of up to five members each.

Time Required

Fifteen to forty minutes.

Materials

Masking tape; a small empty plastic bottle (e.g., soda or dishwashing liquid) to act as a bowling pin; a small amount of sand; five small rubber balls (four of one color and one of another color); a ruler or yardstick.

Preparation

Place a small amount of sand in the bottom of the plastic bottle. Use masking tape to designate a starting line on the floor where the competition will take place. Set the bottle approximately five feet from this line.

Process

1. Instruct participants to form teams of up to five members each. Explain that the object of the game is for each team to work together to get the first ball that is rolled (the odd-colored primary ball) to touch the "pin" (bottle) without knocking it over. Only one team at a time will participate in the competition. The first player from each team will roll the primary ball and then all subsequent team members will try to roll their balls so that they nudge the primary ball closer to the pin, without knocking it over. If the bottle is knocked over at any time during the competition, that team is eliminated.

2. The first team to compete will approach the starting line and the first player begins by rolling the odd-colored primary ball. When all members of the team have rolled their balls, the facilitator will measure how close the primary ball is to the pin.

3. The procedure is repeated with each remaining group. The team that gets the primary ball closest to the pin without knocking it over is the winner.

Discussion

♦ How close was your team to meeting its goal?

♦ What factors affected the final outcome?

♦ What was your team's initial strategy?

♦ How well did the team adjust its approach if the outcome was different than expected (e.g., if the rolled ball missed the primary one or knocked it off course)?

♦ Why is change necessary for continued improvement?

♦ Relate this game to strategic planning in the workplace.

Objective

To form a series of word connections by linking picture symbols.

Applications

♦ Change

♦ Communication

♦ Conflict Resolution

♦ Decision Making

♦ Perception

♦ Resource Use

Group Size

Unlimited. Participants will work in teams of up to ten members each.

Time Required

Fifteen to twenty minutes.

Materials

One envelope containing a set of Pix Cards for each team.

Preparation

For each set of Pix Cards (each team needs a complete set): Duplicate Pix Card Sheets 1-4 on card stock and cut into individual cards following the dashed lines. Place the twenty-four cards in an envelope.

Process

1. Instruct participants to form teams of up to ten members each. Distribute one envelope containing a set of Pix Cards to each team.

2. Explain that each card has a picture on it representing a particular word. The object of the game is to form the longest possible line of picture cards by connecting the ending letter of one word to the beginning letter of another word. For example: a picture of a ROS<u>E</u> would connect to a picture of an <u>E</u>G<u>G</u> which would connect to a picture of a <u>G</u>IRAFFE, and so on. The winning team is the one that is able to form the longest chain of picture cards in a given period of time. Groups will have approximately ten to fifteen minutes for group work.

3. Signal for the activity to begin. When the allotted time period has expired, determine which team has the highest number of linked cards.

Discussion

♦ What role did perception play in this game? (*pictures may represent different words to some people*)

♦ How willing were team members to revise an arrangement in order to try to form a longer chain?

♦ What approach did the group take in deciding how to sequence the words?

♦ Did conflicts arise? How were they resolved?

Pix Cards Sheet 1

Pix Cards Sheet 2

Pix Cards Sheet 3

Pix Cards Sheet 4

29 ◆ Playing for Keeps

Objective

To determine how best to win your opponent's cards by playing your most effective resource.

Applications

◆ Change

◆ Decision Making

◆ Group Interaction

◆ Resource Use

◆ Risk Taking

◆ Strategic Planning

Group Size

Eight to twenty-four participants, who will form two teams of equal size.

Time Required

Fifteen to thirty minutes.

Materials

One deck of playing cards; a flip chart (optional).

Process

1. Instruct participants to form two teams of equal size and assign each team to a different area of the room.

2. Explain that one at a time, each player will draw a card from the shuffled deck of playing cards. Explain that team members will gather together, examine their cards, and plan a strategy for winning "tricks" against the opposing team. A team may alter its strategy as play progresses depending on wins, losses, or the strategy of the other team. The rules for winning tricks are as follows (these rules may be posted on a flip chart):

   ♦ Hearts are considered trump.

   ♦ High card wins unless it is trumped.

   ♦ Same-value cards:

      Clubs win over diamonds or spades.

      Diamonds win over spades.

3. Utilize a coin flip or some other method to determine which team will play the first card. The lead-off player shows a card, followed by the opposing team's player. The winner collects both cards and a brief period is allowed for each team to decide the upcoming play.

4. The next card is played by the second set of players, with the lead-off player from the previous trick's winning team. When everyone has played his or her cards, the team with the most cards wins.

Discussion

♦ How did limited resources (the team's cards) affect planning?

♦ Was it necessary to change the team's initial strategy? Why?

♦ How well did the team adjust its strategy?

♦ What risks, if any, was the team willing to take?

♦ What reactions occurred among members of the team as play progressed?

♦ How does this game relate to strategic planning in the workplace?

30 ◆ Poetic License

Objective

To create short poems from specified words provided by a member of your team.

Applications

◆ Communication

◆ Creativity

◆ Delegation

◆ Icebreaker

Group Size

Unlimited. Participants will work in teams of up to five members each.

Time Required

Five to ten minutes.

Materials

A blank sheet of paper and a pencil for each participant; a clock or timer.

Process

1. Instruct participants to form teams of up to five members each. Distribute a pencil and a blank sheet of paper to each participant.

2. Explain that the object of the activity is for each team member to create a poem using words that will be assigned by another member of the group. Each player will have approximately five minutes to write a poem.

3. Direct each team member to write four rhyming words at the top of a blank sheet of paper. All four words may rhyme (e.g., snow, blow, woe, toe), or they may consist of two pairs of rhyming words (e.g., bad, mad, cheer, here).

4. When individuals have completed the rhyming word assignment, each participant passes his or her paper to the player on the right, who will create a poem using the designated words. The poems should be creative yet logical. Every player should be given a sheet of rhyming words from another player in his or her group.

5. Signal for the activity to begin, and allow approximately five minutes for group work. When all teams have completed the assignment, ask participants to share their poems. Depending on the total number of participants, this may be done within the individual teams or with the reassembled total group.

Discussion

♦ How did you feel about assigning the rhyming words to another member of your team?

♦ How difficult was this game? Why?

♦ In the workplace, why is it important to combine creativity with logical thinking?

31 ◆ Puzzling

Objective

To assemble a jigsaw puzzle in successive stages with other team players.

Applications

◆ Delegation

◆ Goals

◆ Icebreaker

◆ Problem Solving

◆ Resource Use

◆ Team Effort

Group Size

Six to fifty participants, who will form teams of equal size.

Time Required

Five to ten minutes.

Materials

Several jigsaw puzzles of twelve or more pieces each (each team needs a complete puzzle); masking tape.

Preparation

Place the pieces of each disassembled puzzle in a loose pile on a table, keeping sufficient space between the team puzzles. For each team, use masking tape to mark a starting point on the floor that is at least ten feet away from the team's puzzle. Allow sufficient room behind the tape for the participants to form a line facing the puzzle on the table.

Process

1. Instruct the participants to form as many equal-size teams as the number of puzzles. Then the members of each group form a line, one behind the other, facing the puzzle pieces at one of the starting lines on the floor. Explain that each team is to work together to assemble one jigsaw puzzle according to the procedures described below. The first team to complete the entire puzzle is the winner.

   The first player on each team runs forward to the puzzle and puts any two pieces together. Then the player returns to his or her group and tags the next player, who runs to the puzzle and puts an additional two pieces together. This procedure continues until the team completes its puzzle.

2. Signal for the activity to begin. Allow enough time for all teams to complete the task and note the order in which teams finish. The first team to complete the entire puzzle is the winner.

Discussion:

♦ How did each member's achievement contribute to the whole?

♦ How does breaking down a project into smaller parts help in goal setting?

♦ What similarities does this have to delegation?

♦ What impact did the diminishing number of pieces have on completing the puzzle?

♦ How did the team react as the puzzle neared completion? (*Generally we work harder as the goal gets closer.*)

32 ◆ Reflections

Objective

To use mirrors to relay a beam of light from one team member to another.

Applications

- ◆ Creativity
- ◆ Icebreaker
- ◆ Leadership
- ◆ Problem Solving
- ◆ Team Effort

Group Size

Four to thirty-six participants, who will work in teams of four to six members each.

Time Required

Approximately ten minutes.

Materials

A small pocket mirror for each participant; a flashlight for each team; index cards (one card for each flashlight); tape; scissors.

Preparation

Obtain enough materials to provide one mirror for each participant and one flashlight for each team. The flashlights need to be sufficiently high-powered to provide a strong beam. To narrow the light and allow a smaller beam to escape, tape an index card with a small slit cut in the center over the face of the flashlight. *Variation*: If conditions allow, a beam of sunlight may be substituted for the flashlight (see Note in the Process section).

Process

1. Instruct participants to form teams of four to six members each and to stand in a circle. Select one person from each group to act as the team leader.

2. Distribute one flashlight to each team leader and a mirror to all remaining participants. (If sunlight is used instead of a flashlight, each participant receives a mirror.)

3. Explain that the objective for each group is to use the mirrors to transmit the light beam around the circle until it returns to the beginning. The leader will direct the light to one player's mirror, who will in turn direct it to the next team member. This continues until the beam has been reflected to all the mirrors and returns to shine on the leader's flashlight.

   Note: If sunlight is used as the source of light, the team leader must use a mirror to catch the initial beam and send it to the next player. The circuit is complete when the light is reflected back to the leader's mirror.

4. Signal for the activity to begin. Allow approximately five minutes for groups to work on this activity, noting which teams were able to accomplish the task.

Discussion

♦ What approach did the group take to accomplish the task?

♦ What factors influenced the team's ability to succeed?

♦ How did each team member's achievement contribute to the overall effort?

♦ How important was the role of the leader?

♦ How does this game relate to teamwork in general?

33 ◆ Rocket Race

Objective

To design and construct a balloon rocket that can carry a paper sheet the longest distance.

Applications

- ◆ Change
- ◆ Creativity
- ◆ Group Interaction
- ◆ Problem Solving
- ◆ Resource Use
- ◆ Risk Taking

Group Size

Six to thirty-five participants, who will work in teams of up to five members each.

Time Required

Twenty to thirty minutes.

Materials

One sausage-shaped balloon, five blank sheets of paper, and a straw for each participating team; tape; scissors; twenty-five to thirty feet of string (or fishing line).

Preparation

For each participating team, obtain one set of the following materials: a balloon, a straw, and five blank sheets of paper. Place the tape and scissors in an area accessible to all teams. Hold the string for the rocket launch.

Process

1. Instruct participants to form several teams, with a maximum of five members on each team. Distribute one set of materials to each group.

2. Explain that the goal for each team is to construct a balloon rocket that will carry one full sheet of paper as far as possible along a string (or fishing line). Teams can use only the materials they were given plus the tape and scissors that are accessible to all groups. Groups will have ten minutes to determine the best way to build the rocket (how to fold the paper and attach it to a balloon, how to attach the balloon to a straw). Teams may not alter their entry in any way once the design time expires.

   Each team will take a turn at launching its balloon rocket. Two participants should hold the ends of the string (or fishing line). The member representing the competing group is to slip the straw onto one end of the string and release the air from the balloon at the appropriate signal.

3. Signal for the activity to begin. Each group will make one attempt, in turn, at launching its rocket. The team whose balloon rocket travels the greatest distance is the winner.

Solution

Participants should consider the best way to fold or crumple the sheet of paper (e.g., make a paper airplane or fold the paper into long, thin strips) as well as the best way to attach the balloon to the straw (the balloon should not be taped to the full length of the straw because of shrinkage as air escapes).

Discussion

♦ In what ways did your team make use of its members' collective skills?

♦ How successful was your team in making the most effective use of the materials?

♦ How did your group test its rocket design?

♦ What, if any, design changes were implemented?

♦ How can we use the process of experimentation to minimize risks?

♦ Relate this game to project management in the workplace.

34 ◆ Roundabout

Objective

To use clues to solve a seating arrangement logic problem with your team.

Applications

◆ Conflict Resolution

◆ Data Analysis

◆ Decision Making

◆ Group Interaction

◆ Problem Solving

Group Size

Unlimited. Participants will work in teams of up to six members each.

Time Required

Fifteen to thirty minutes.

Materials

A set of Roundabout Worksheet cards in an envelope for each team; one copy of the Roundabout Solution Sheet for each team.

Preparation

Duplicate the Roundabout Worksheet on card stock, making one copy for each participating team. Cut each copy into individual cards along the dashed lines, and place the entire set of cards in an envelope. Each team will receive an envelope with a complete set of cards. Also duplicate a copy of the Roundabout Solution Sheet on regular copier paper for each team.

Process

1. Instruct participants to form teams of up to six members each. Distribute one envelope filled with one set of cards to each group and assign the groups to work in separate areas of the training room.

2. Read the following scenario to the participants:

    > Recently, a group of friends got together to play cards. As they arrived, each person greeted the hostess and then took a seat at a large round table. The next morning, Tina was trying to recall exactly where everyone had been seated. She decided to list some of the events that had occurred to help herself remember. Can you help Tina reconstruct the seating arrangements?

    Explain that each team needs to determine Tina's correct seating arrangement using the clue cards provided in the envelope.

3. Allow sufficient time (approximately ten to fifteen minutes) for the groups to work together to determine the circular seating arrangement.

4. Distribute one copy of the Roundabout Solution Sheet to each team and instruct them to check their answer for accuracy. Using a show of hands, determine how many teams were able to solve the problem correctly.

Discussion

♦ How well did team members work together?

♦ How well did your team do in solving the actual problem?

♦ What approach did your team take to arrive at its solution?

♦ What factors influenced your final outcome?

♦ How were differences of opinion or conflicts resolved?

♦ Did the order in which you used the information cards influence the outcome? How?

♦ How can a systematic approach to analyzing data help in solving problems in the workplace?

Roundabout Worksheet

May was flirting with both men who were seated on either side of her.

Annie had turned to her left to talk to her friend June about the weather.

There were exactly three people sitting between May and June.

Augie was sitting directly across from Tim, and Max was to the right of May.

June sat two places, going counterclockwise, from Julio's seat.

Julio and Tim were sitting next to another man at the table.

ANNIE	**AUGIE**
JUNE	**JULIO**
MAY	**MAX**
TINA	**TIM**

Roundabout Solution Sheet

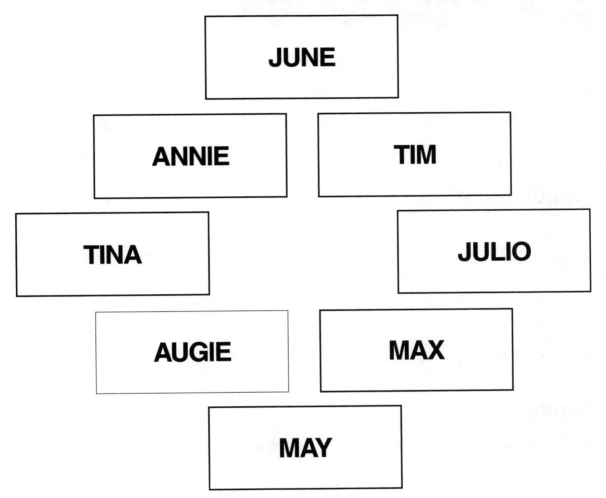

1) June is on Annie's left
2) There are 3 people sitting between May and June
   (Halfway - opposite from each other)
3) Max is on May's right
4) May is sitting between two men *(Either Augie, Tim, or Julio)*
5) June is sitting two places, counterclockwise, from Julio
6) Julio and Tim are sitting next to another man
7) Augie is directly across from Tim *(Augie is across from Tim so he can't be **next** to Julio)*
8) Place Tina in the last vacant position

35 ♦ Sales Pitch

Objective

To work in teams developing a commercial advertisement using a specified mix of words.

Applications

♦ Communication

♦ Creativity

♦ Group Interaction

♦ Perception

♦ Team Effort

Group Size

Five to thirty participants, who will work in teams of up to five members each.

Time Required

Thirty to forty-five minutes.

Materials

Ten blank index cards and a felt-tip marker for each group; four small empty boxes (or bags) to hold the word cards; one sheet of newsprint for each group; a flip chart.

Preparation

On each of the four boxes (or bags), use a felt-tip marker to indicate a single word category—Noun, Adverb, Verb, and Adjective. Then prepare a flip chart showing these numbers and categories:

1 Noun

2 Adverbs

3 Verbs

4 Adjectives

Process

1. Instruct participants to form teams of up to five members each. Distribute ten blank index cards and a felt-tip marker to each group.

2. Referring to the prepared flip chart, explain that each team is to think of the designated *number* of words shown next to each word *category*. Only one word should be written on each of the ten cards provided, and the cards for each category should be kept separate.

3. Allow approximately five minutes for the groups to work on this assignment.

4. At the end of the designated time period, collect all the cards, placing them in the appropriate labeled boxes or bags. Place the boxes (or bags) in a central location.

5. Explain that the teams will be creating commercial advertisements. These ads will involve a specific object that will be described using the designated words, randomly chosen by the group. Distribute one sheet of newsprint to each team. Ask a representative from each group to choose one noun card, two adverb cards, three verb cards, and four adjective cards from the appropriate boxes of cards. The words selected should be written on each team's sheet of newsprint.

6. Explain that each team needs to develop a commercial advertisement about the object (the noun) that convincingly persuades someone to buy it. The commercial should meet the following specifications: (1) it should last no more than two minutes; (2) all the selected words should be used appropriately; (3) it must be

convincing; and (4) it must involve all team members. Each presenting group will be evaluated using this criteria by all the remaining observer teams.

7. Allow approximately fifteen minutes for group work. Then ask each team to display its newsprint sheet before presenting its commercial to the total group. The observer teams will judge whether or not the commercial met all the appropriate specifications.

Discussion

♦ How did you feel about having other teams judge your work?

♦ How difficult was it to effectively use the selected words?

♦ What part of the commercials made the message believable?

♦ How does the *way* in which we communicate affect the opinion of others?

♦ What impact does this have on situations in the workplace?

36 ♦ Scavenger Search

Objective

To find specified items from among your personal possessions.

Applications

♦ Communication

♦ Icebreaker

♦ Perception

♦ Self-Disclosure

Group Size

Unlimited. Participants will work in teams of up to ten members each, with a minimum of two teams.

Time Required

Five to ten minutes.

Materials

A Scavenger Search item list; a flip chart; a felt-tip marker.

Preparation

Prepare a list of items that are commonly found in an individual's possession. A sample list may include the following: a pencil, a penny dated before 1975, a picture of a family member, a nail file, a mirror, a notepad, a calendar, etc. (Try not to select items that are predominantly carried by members of only one gender.)

Process

1. Instruct participants to form a minimum of two teams of up to ten members each. Designate an identifying group number or color for each team.

2. Explain that you have a prepared list of common items that participants may have in their possession. Everyone on the team participates. As each item is announced, the first team to hold up that object is awarded one point. The team with the highest number of points at the end of the game is the winner.

3. One by one, call out the items on your Scavenger Search item list. Record team scores on the flip chart as each point is awarded. After the entire list has been read, the team with the highest total number of points is the winner.

Discussion

♦ How do personal possessions act as an indicator of someone's interests?

♦ How does individual perception relate to this process?

♦ What assumptions can be made as a result of individual perception?

37 ◆ Ship Ahoy

Objective

To work together to lead and maneuver a blindfolded "boat" from one destination to another without a collision.

Applications

◆ Communication

◆ Group Interaction

◆ Icebreaker

◆ Leadership

◆ Team Effort

◆ Trust

Group Size

Five to twenty participants.

Time Required

Five to ten minutes.

Materials

A blindfold; masking tape.

Preparation

Mark the activity's starting and ending points with masking tape on the floor.

Process

1. Explain that the objective of the activity is for the group as a whole to maneuver a "boat" (a blindfolded person) from one port to another without bumping into the other boats (the remaining group members).

2. Select one individual to become the transport (or lead) boat and place the blindfold on this player. Lead the individual to the starting point.

3. Explain that the lead boat is not allowed to touch any of the other boats while traveling to the other port because each collision will result in extensive damage. Visually indicate the final port (marked by masking tape) to the remaining participants, who are then distributed throughout the area; these group members act as boats in the harbor that will guide the transport boat to its final destination. Explain that as the lead boat approaches, the nearest boat will start beeping like a foghorn to avoid collision. The transport boat (the blindfolded player) then approaches slowly and attempts to maneuver through without bumping into another boat.

4. Signal for the activity to begin and monitor progress.

Discussion

♦ How effective were the harbor boats in leading the transport boat?

♦ How did the individual representing the transport boat feel about being directed by everyone else?

♦ How effective was the communication process (the warning beeps)?

♦ What role did group size play in this game?

♦ Relate this game to teamwork in general.

38 ◆ Sign Language

Objective

To design informational signs using only symbols, not words.

Applications

◆ Communication

◆ Creativity

◆ Diversity

◆ Group Interaction

◆ Perception

◆ Sales

Group Size

Five to fifty participants, who will work in teams of up to six members each.

Time Required

Twenty to forty-five minutes.

Materials

Five sheets of newsprint and an assortment of felt-tip markers for each team; a flip chart.

Preparation

Prepare a flip chart with the following information:

- ♦ Administration

- ♦ Customs

- ♦ First Aid

- ♦ Ticket Information

Process

1. Instruct participants to form teams of up to six members each. Distribute five sheets of newsprint paper and a variety of felt-tip markers to each participating team.

2. Explain that each group's task is to design a total of four information signs for use in a new international airport. To overcome language barriers, the signs should convey their message by simple symbols, **without words.** The signs must be clear, distinctive, and easy to remember. It is essential that the signs be easily understood because they will be used to direct people to the facilities and not necessarily posted on the actual agency door.

   Referring to the prepared flip chart, reveal the four agency signs that are to be designed by each team. Explain that teams will have approximately twenty minutes to complete the activity.

3. Signal for the activity to begin and allow twenty minutes for teams to complete the assignment.

4. Have each team present its signs to the rest of the audience. You may wish to post the signs around the room, having the team members group them according to agency designation.

Discussion

- ♦ How did your team work together to share ideas?

- ♦ What were some similarities shared by various agency signs?

- Are the signs easy to interpret? Why?

- How does language (communication) impact our daily activities?

- How are symbols used in sales advertising?

- What impact will the global economy have on future business exchanges?

- How can we improve our communication processes?

39 ♦ Skyscrapers

Objective

To build the highest freestanding structure from drinking straws.

Applications

♦ Creativity

♦ Diversity

♦ Group Interaction

♦ Negotiation

♦ Problem Solving

♦ Resource Use

Group Size

Unlimited. Participants will work in teams of up to six members each.

Time Required

Thirty to forty-five minutes.

Materials

Drinking straws (a set of twenty-five to thirty per team); an assortment of tape, pins, paper clips, rubber bands; a ruler or yardstick; a clock with a second hand or a timer.

Preparation

Bundle the straws into sets of twenty-five to thirty per team. Place all the remaining objects, except the ruler and clock, on a table that is accessible to all groups.

Process

1. Instruct the participants to form teams of up to six members each. Explain that each team will attempt to construct a freestanding framework that is taller than any other team's structure. Each group will receive a set of straws with which to build the structure, and everyone will share access to various other supplies. The facilitator may wish to allow teams to discover how to join the straws; alternatively, the facilitator can demonstrate some of the ways in which the straws can be joined:

   Squeeze one end of a straw and place it inside another straw; use pins or tape to hold straws together; bind straws where they intersect with rubber bands; or put them together with paper clips, as shown below.

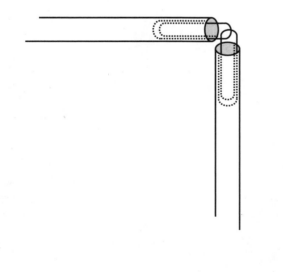

2. Distribute one set of straws to each team and indicate the location of the other supplies. Explain that the time limit for construction is twenty minutes, and the team with the highest *freestanding* structure will be the winner.

3. Signal for the activity to begin. Five minutes before the time expires, announce a five-minute warning. At the end of the twenty-minute work period, the facilitator should measure all structures to determine the tallest skyscraper. While this is being done, discuss and compare the various ways in which the structures have been built. The team with the tallest skyscraper is the winner.

Discussion

♦ In your opinion, which structure was the most creative?

♦ How do things that look different in the workplace still serve similar functions?

♦ How did your team come up with a plan for the structure?

♦ How well did team members work together?

♦ If conflicts arose, how were they resolved?

♦ How did you feel about sharing resources with other teams?

♦ Did you need to negotiate with other teams for use of the shared supplies? How effective were the negotiations?

40 ♦ Soccer Fan

Objective

To compete against another team by fanning a ball into the goal box to achieve the highest point score.

Applications

♦ Goals

♦ Group Interaction

♦ Leadership

♦ Planning

♦ Team Effort

Group Size

Six to thirty participants. This game requires an even number of groups of up to five members each, who will compete in paired teams.

Time Required

Fifteen to twenty minutes.

Materials

One Soccer Fan Instructions Sheet and a stapler for each participating team; blank sheets of paper (at least one sheet per participant); ping pong balls or small styrofoam balls (one ball for each pair of teams); small boxes (one for each team); masking tape.

Preparation

For each pair of participating teams, prepare a playing area as follows: Tape the side of one small box to each of the opposite ends of a table so that the opening is facing up and level with the table top. Place a piece of masking tape in the center of the table midway between the ends. (See diagrams below, showing side and top views.)

Process

1. Instruct participants to form an even number of teams (i.e., 2, 4, 6, etc.) of up to five members each, and pair the teams for competition. Each team will select one member to act as goalkeeper.

2. Provide a stapler and one copy of the Soccer Fan Instructions Sheet to each team. Distribute one blank sheet of paper to each participant. Review the instructions with the participants and allow approximately five minutes for team members to construct the paper fans.

3. Position each pair of teams around a prepared playing area, with the goalkeepers placed at their own team's "goal box." Provide each table with one ball, which is to be placed on the tape mark in the center of the table. Explain that team members will use their fans to propel the ball toward their team's goal box while trying to prevent the other team from doing the same. Each time the ball enters the appropriate box, that team scores one point. If the ball goes off the table, it is considered a foul and play resumes with the ball placed on the center tape mark.

4. Allow approximately ten minutes for the competition. Each team's goalkeepers should keep score. Determine the winning teams after obtaining feedback on the total points scored.

Discussion

♦ Did your team perform as well as you expected? Why?

♦ What strategies did your team use?

♦ How were leadership roles assumed?

♦ What was the importance of each player to the team effort?

♦ Did each player participate at the same level? Why?

♦ Relate this game to project planning in the workplace.

Soccer Fan Instructions Sheet

To form fans, fold a sheet of paper at 1-inch intervals, alternating folds in opposite directions. Gather together at one end and staple. (*See illustration below.*)

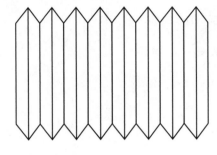 

41 ♦ Sporting Chance

Objective

To identify the names of twenty sporting activities with only the vowels provided for each.

Applications

♦ Data Analysis

♦ Icebreaker

♦ Leadership

♦ Team Effort

♦ Time Pressure

Group Size

Unlimited. Participants will work in teams of up to five members each.

Time Required

Five to ten minutes.

Materials

A pencil and a copy of the Sporting Chance Worksheet for each participating team; a Sporting Chance Solution Sheet; a clock or timer.

Process

1. Instruct participants to form teams of up to five members each and select one group member from each team to act as leader. Distribute a pencil and one copy of the Sporting Chance Worksheet to each team leader.

2. Explain that group members will work together to complete the list of words, each representing the name of a sporting event. The vowels have been provided for each word, and the team must determine the appropriate consonants, one per space. The team leader, who is responsible for recording the letters, will stand when the task is complete. The team that correctly completes the worksheet in the shortest amount of time will be declared the winner.

3. Signal for the activity to begin. The facilitator should note the order in which teams complete the activity. Stop the activity after five minutes have elapsed, even if a group is still working. Review the answers to the worksheet using participant feedback and the Sporting Chance Solution Sheet provided. Determine the highest number of correct answers, then declare the winning team based on the highest score and the shortest amount of time for completion.

Discussion

♦ What factors influenced your ability to complete the task? (*Knowledge of sports, time pressure, group size, etc.*)

♦ How could your team have improved its performance?

♦ What role, if any, did the team leader assume in addition to that of recordkeeper?

♦ How did time pressure affect group member interaction?

♦ What sports rely heavily on teamwork in order to perform well?

♦ How are work teams similar to athletic teams?

Sporting Chance Worksheet

Complete the following words by adding consonants to name 20 sporting events.

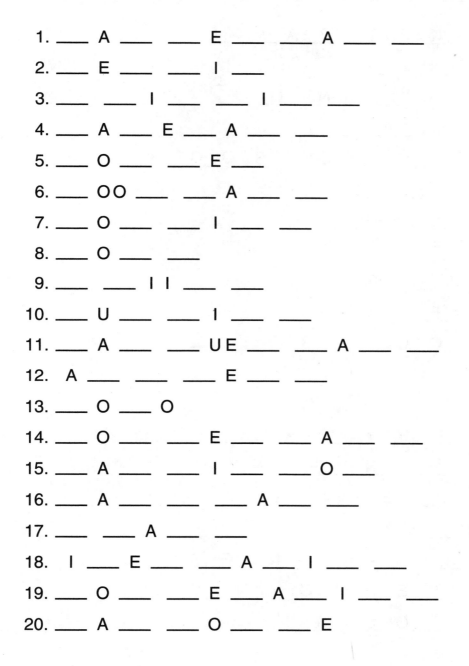

1. __ A __ __ E __ __ A __ __
2. __ E __ __ I __
3. __ __ I __ __ I __ __
4. __ A __ E __ A __ __
5. __ O __ __ E __
6. __ OO __ __ A __ __
7. __ O __ __ I __ __
8. __ O __ __
9. __ __ I I __ __
10. __ U __ __ I __ __
11. __ A __ __ U E __ __ A __ __
12. A __ __ __ E __ __
13. __ O __ O
14. __ O __ __ E __ __ A __ __
15. __ A __ __ I __ __ O __
16. __ A __ __ __ A __ __
17. __ __ A __ __
18. I __ E __ __ A __ I __ __
19. __ O __ __ E __ A __ I __ __
20. __ A __ __ O __ __ E

Sporting Chance Solution Sheet

1. B A S K E T B A L L
2. T E N N I S
3. S W I M M I N G
4. B A S E B A L L
5. H O C K E Y **OR** S O C C E R
6. F OO T B A L L
7. B O W L I N G
8. G O L F
9. S K I I N G
10. S U R F I N G
11. R A C Q U E T B A L L
12. A R C H E R Y
13. P O L O
14. V O L L E Y B A L L
15. B A D M I N T O N
16. H A N D B A L L
17. T R A C K
18. I C E S K A T I N G
19. H O R S E R A C I N G
20. L A C R O S S E

42 ◆ Square Off

Objective

To compete in a live tic-tac-toe game.

Applications

◆ Conflict Resolution

◆ Decision Making

◆ Group Interaction

◆ Icebreaker

◆ Leadership

◆ Strategic Planning

Group Size

Eight to fifty participants. This game requires an even number of groups of four or five members each, who will compete in paired teams.

Time Required

Approximately ten minutes.

Materials

Masking tape.

Preparation

For each pair of competing teams: Use masking tape to create a large tic-tac-toe diagram on the floor, as shown in the illustration below. Each cell within the diagram should be approximately 18 inches square.

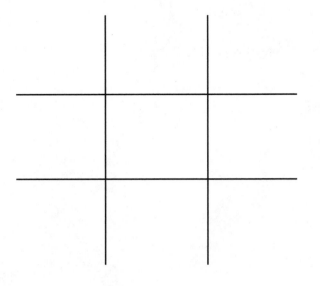

Process

1. Instruct participants to form paired teams of four or five members each. Select one member from each team to act as team leader.

2. Explain that each pair of teams will compete in a live tic-tac-toe game. One team will be the "Crosses" (X's) and the other will be the "Circles" (O's). The leaders from each competing team will determine the team designations.

3. When the signal is given, the leader from the Circle team will take a position in any one of the squares of the diagram. Next, the leader of the Cross team will take a position in another square. Then players from each side will take turns placing themselves in squares in an attempt to win the game of tic-tac-toe. A win occurs when there are three players from the same team standing in a row, either straight or diagonally. Teams are to continue playing until a signal is given to stop. Leaders will keep track of the number of games won by their team.

4. Signal for the activity to begin and allow approximately five minutes for teams to compete. Determine the winner for each competing pair of teams.

Discussion

◆ How did the team plan its playing strategy?

◆ What factors influenced your team's plans as the game progressed?

◆ What impact did they have?

◆ How cooperatively did opposing team members act when "squaring off" in the diagram cells?

◆ What role did the team leaders play overall?

43 ◆ State of the Union

Objective

To reach a team goal of correct associations for states with their appropriate nickname, bird, flower, and motto.

Applications

◆ Data Analysis

◆ Decision Making

◆ Goal Setting

◆ Group Interaction

◆ Leadership

Group Size

Unlimited. Participants will work in teams of up to five members each.

Time Required

Twenty to thirty minutes.

Materials

A pencil and one copy each of the State of the Union Handout and the State of the Union Chart for each participant; one copy of the State of the Union Answer Sheet for each team.

Process

1. Instruct participants to form teams of up to five members each. Have each team select a leader who will be responsible for coordinating group work and recording the team's answers. Distribute a pencil and one copy each of the State of the Union Handout and the State of the Union Chart to each participant.

2. Explain that teams will use the Handout to choose the appropriate nickname, bird, flower, and motto for each state listed on the Chart. Before proceeding, each group must predict how many correct answers out of the possible forty-eight it will correctly determine. This number should be placed in the upper-right corner of the team leader's copy of the State of the Union Chart.

3. Allow approximately ten to fifteen minutes for group work. When all teams have finished, distribute one copy of the State of the Union Answer Sheet to each team leader. Teams are to score their charts using this sheet, entering the number of actual correct answers under the prediction. Determine which team had the highest overall number of correct answers.

Discussion

♦ How close did your team come in predicting the number of correct answers? Better or worse?

♦ On what basis were your predictions made?

♦ How were you able to progressively build on your use of the information provided? (As *information is used, additional connections can be made.*)

♦ What role did the leader take in the decision-making process?

♦ How did the size of the group affect decision making?

State of the Union Handout

NICKNAMES

Badger State	Land of Enchantment
Beehive State	Land of Opportunity
First State	Peach State
Granite State	Sagebrush State
Jayhawk State	Sooner State
Keystone State	Tarheel State

FLOWERS

Apple Blossom	Purple Lilac
Cherokee Rose	Sagebrush
Dogwood	Sego Lily
Mistletoe	Sunflower
Mountain Laurel	Wood Violet
Peach Blossom	Yucca

BIRDS

Blue Hen Chicken	Roadrunner
Brown Thrasher	Robin
Cardinal	Ruffed Grouse
Mockingbird	Scissor-tailed Flycatcher
Mountain Bluebird	Seagull
Purple Finch	Western Meadowlark

MOTTOS

All for our country	Live free or die
Forward	The people rule
Industry	To be rather than to seem
It grows as it goes	To the stars through difficulties
Labor conquers all things	Virtue, liberty and independence
Liberty and independence	Wisdom, justice, and moderation

State of the Union Chart

STATE	NICKNAME	FLOWER	BIRD	MOTTO
Arkansas				
Delaware				
Georgia				
Kansas				
Nevada				
New Hampshire				
New Mexico				
North Carolina				
Oklahoma				
Pennsylvania				
Utah				
Wisconsin				

State of the Union Answer Sheet

STATE	NICKNAME	FLOWER	BIRD	MOTTO
Arkansas	Land of Opportunity	Apple Blossom	Mockingbird	The people rule
Delaware	First State	Peach Blossom	Blue Hen Chicken	Liberty and independence
Georgia	Peach State	Cherokee Rose	Brown Thrasher	Wisdom, justice, and moderation
Kansas	Jayhawk State	Sunflower	Western Meadowlark	To the stars through difficulties
Nevada	Sagebrush State	Sagebrush	Mountain Bluebird	All for our country
New Hampshire	Granite State	Purple Lilac	Purple Finch	Live free or die
New Mexico	Land of Enchantment	Yucca	Roadrunner	It grows as it goes
North Carolina	Tarheel State	Dogwood	Cardinal	To be rather than to seem
Oklahoma	Sooner State	Mistletoe	Scissor-tailed Flycatcher	Labor conquers all things
Pennsylvania	Keystone State	Mountain Laurel	Ruffed Grouse	Virtue, liberty, and independence
Utah	Beehive State	Sego Lily	Seagull	Industry
Wisconsin	Badger State	Wood Violet	Robin	Forward

44 ◆ Story Time

Objective

To explore the different ways teams can create a story using the same designated word list.

Applications

◆ Communication

◆ Creativity

◆ Diversity

◆ Leadership

◆ Problem Solving

◆ Resource Use

Group Size

Six to forty participants, who will work in teams of three or four members each.

Time Required

Twenty to thirty minutes.

Materials

A pencil and one copy of the Story Time Worksheet for each participant.

Process

1. Instruct participants to form teams of three to four members each. Group leadership is assigned to the person with the most recent birthday (or some other designation). Distribute a pencil and one copy of the Story Time Worksheet to each participant.

2. Explain that each team will create a story that uses all of the words presented in the table. Each word may be used only once; the only words that may be added are verbs (e.g., *elect, push, drove*), articles (e.g., *the, a, an*), and prepositions (e.g., *of, for, from, with*). The team leader is responsible for coordinating the process and presenting the final story.

3. Signal for the activity to begin, and allow approximately fifteen minutes for group work. Give a five-minute warning before time is up. Have each leader read his or her team's story before the total group and compare stories for similarities and differences.

Discussion

♦ How do we account for the different story lines that resulted from the exact same word base?

♦ How do these differences relate to diversity in the workplace?

♦ What problem-solving process did the team use to approach the task?

♦ Was it effective? Why?

♦ What role did perception play in this game?

♦ How did the leader feel about his or her role in the group?

♦ How difficult was it to complete this activity within the constraints presented?

♦ Relate this activity to the use of limited resources in the workplace.

Story Time Worksheet

Create a logical story that uses ALL of the words presented in the table below. You are limited to adding only verbs, articles, and prepositions.

motorcycle	ice	girll	police officer
sidewalk	driver	book	ketchup
President	tree	boy	teddy bear
computer	shoes	baby	diploma
mouse	radio	lion	parking lot

45 ◆ Structural Changes

Objective

To compete against other teams forming four different shapes from identical pattern pieces.

Applications

◆ Change

◆ Diversity

◆ Group Interaction

◆ Problem Solving

◆ Risk Taking

◆ Time Pressure

Group Size

Eight to fifty participants, who will work in teams of four or five members each.

Time Required

Ten to twenty minutes.

Materials

One envelope containing a set of Structural Changes puzzle pieces and one copy of the Structural Changes Solutions Sheet for each participating team; scissors; a stopwatch or a clock with a second hand; a flip chart (optional).

Preparation

For each participating team: Duplicate four copies of the Structural Changes Puzzle on card stock. Cut each of the four puzzles into separate pieces and place all the pieces into one envelope. Also duplicate one copy of the Structural Changes Solutions Sheet on regular copier stock for each team.

Process

1. Instruct participants to form teams of four or five members each. Distribute one envelope of puzzle pieces to each group.

2. Explain that each envelope contains pattern pieces that will form four distinct structures: a **triangle**, a **square**, a **rectangle**, and a **cross.** When a team completes all four puzzles, group members should raise their hands. The team that completes all four puzzles correctly in the least amount of time will be the winner.

3. Signal for the activity to begin. Record the completion time for each team on a flip chart or a sheet of paper. When all teams have finished, distribute one copy of the Structural Changes Solutions Sheet to each group. Get feedback from each team on whether it correctly constructed the four required shapes, review this against the recorded completion times, and announce the winning team.

Discussion

♦ How well did team members cooperate with one another during the activity?

♦ What problem-solving approach did your team take? (E.*g., divide into four sets of identical pieces.*)

♦ How willing were team members to risk changing the arrangement of puzzle pieces as the task progressed?

♦ Each structure is formed from an identical set of five pattern pieces. Relate this concept to team diversity. (*Each piece is important to form the whole, different formations made from similar pieces, etc.*)

Structural Changes Puzzle

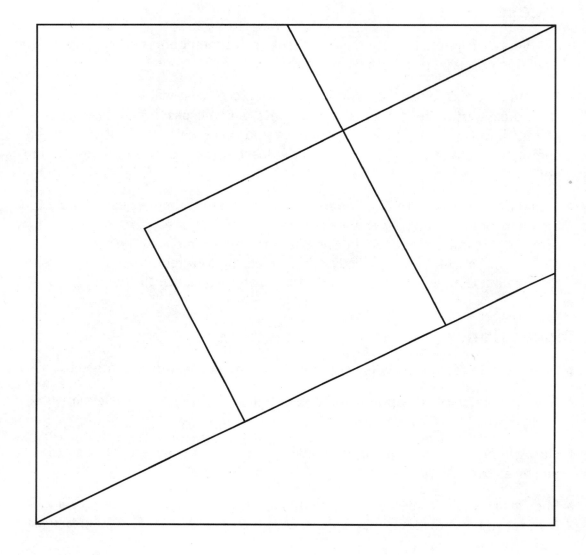

Structural Changes
Solution Sheet

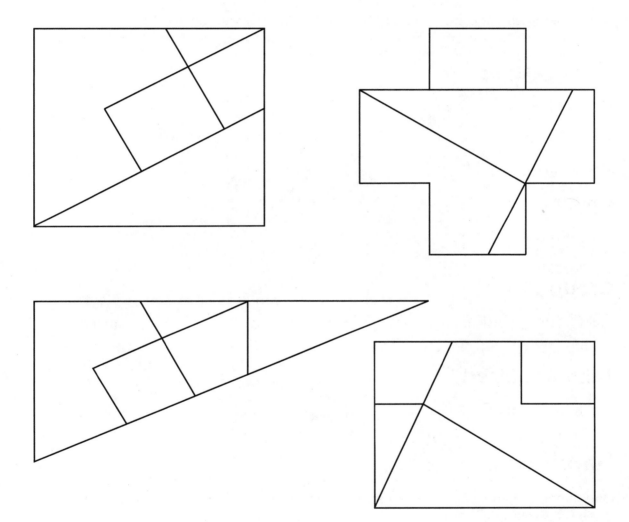

46 ♦ Strung Out

Objective

To compete against other teams in blowing a paper cup along a string.

Applications

♦ Communication (variation)

♦ Icebreaker

♦ Team Effort

♦ Time Pressure

♦ Trust (variation)

Group Size

Eight to thirty participants. This activity requires at least two teams of equal size.

Time Required

Five to ten minutes.

Materials

One paper cup and fifteen feet of string for each team; a pencil; masking tape. *Variation*: blindfolds.

Preparation

Prepare one cup/string set-up for each participating team: Using a pencil, punch a hole in the bottom of a paper cup. Place the cup on a piece of string approximately fifteen feet long. (The actual length of the string will depend on the width limitations of the room.) At a height of approximately five feet, support the string between two objects or attach the ends to opposite walls with tape. Allow sufficient space between team string set-ups for participants to move about freely.

Process

1. Instruct participants to form a minimum of two teams of equal size. Have each group stand at the end (or to the side) of one of the string sets, with team members forming a line. Explain that the teams will compete against each other in a relay race.

2. When the signal is given, the first player on each team will blow the paper cup from the starting point to the other end of the string (the finish line). After the paper cup reaches the end of the string, the player will slide the cup back to the original starting line for the next player to blow across the string. This procedure repeats until all members of the team have participated. If a string becomes dislodged, the current player must reattach it and begin again from the starting point. The team that finishes first is the winner.

3. Signal for the activity to begin. Monitor the teams' progress, and stop the activity when the first team has finished and is announced the winner.

Variation

Blindfold the first competing player from each group and have him or her try to blow the cup along the team's string while blindfolded. The other team members can help instruct the player on how best to blow the cup to the finish line. The cup is returned to the starting line and the blindfold is handed over to the next player, who will repeat the procedure until the cup reaches the end. This continues until all team members have participated.

Discussion

♦ How did the concept of a race (time pressure) affect overall performance?

♦ What impact did the structure itself (string height and distance, cup size, etc.) have on task performance?

♦ (Variation) How well were instructions communicated by team members? How did the interaction affect your level of trust?

47 ◆ Toss-Up

Objective

To cooperate as a team in finding the best way to force a balloon through a hole in a blanket.

Applications

◆ Communication

◆ Group Interaction

◆ Icebreaker

◆ Team Effort

◆ Time Pressure

Group Size

Eight to twenty-four participants, who will work in teams of four members each.

Time Required

Five to twenty minutes.

Materials

Several round balloons; a blanket (or a sheet or plastic cover); a stopwatch or clock with a second hand.

Preparation

Cut a hole *slightly* larger than the size of a round, inflated balloon in the blanket (or in the sheet or plastic). The hole should be cut off-center and to one side. Inflate several balloons and tie off their ends.

Process

1. Instruct participants to form teams of four members each. Explain that the object of the activity is for team members to work together to get a balloon to fall through the hole by manipulating the blanket (or sheet or plastic) as a group. The team that accomplishes this task in the shortest period of time will be the winner.

2. One team at a time will have a chance to compete. Hand the blanket to the first participating group and have each team member take hold of one corner. Place a balloon near the edge opposite the hole and begin timing the task. If the balloon falls off the blanket during play, the facilitator will retrieve it and once again place it at an edge opposite the hole. Timing will stop only when the balloon passes through the hole and hits the ground.

3. Record the elapsed time for each team's effort. After all teams have participated, announce the team with the winning time.

Discussion

♦ How difficult was it to coordinate your team's efforts?

♦ How effectively did team members communicate with one another during the activity?

♦ How did time pressure affect the team's ability to execute the task efficiently?

♦ What role did each individual play in the overall team effort?

♦ What, if anything, could have been done to improve performance?

48 ♦ Treasure Map

Objective

To provide clear, written directions to help guide a team member in locating a treasure on a map.

Applications

♦ Communication

♦ Data Analysis

♦ Leadership

♦ Problem Solving

♦ Strategic Planning

Group Size

Eight to twenty participants, who will work in teams of up to six members each.

Time Required

Twenty to thirty minutes.

Materials

Several blank sheets of letter-size paper and one large sheet of newsprint or drawing paper for each team; a pencil for each participant; a set of crayons for each team (optional); a clock or timer.

Process

1. Instruct participants to form a minimum of two teams of up to six members each, and assign each group to a different area of the room. Distribute one large sheet of newsprint to each team and one pencil to each participant. (Crayons are optional.)

2. Explain that each team will have approximately ten minutes to create a "treasure map." The maps may be as elaborate as the team desires, including trails, mountains, towns, lakes, etc., but should *not* show where a treasure is located. When the map details have been completed, each team should make a small spot on its map and mark it as the starting point.

3. Allow approximately ten minutes for the teams to create their maps.

4. Direct each group to choose one team member to be its "treasure hunter"; these players are instructed to leave the room. Each team then chooses another player to go to an opposing team's map and to name a spot for that team's "treasure" to be located. *No mark is to be made on the opposing team's map*; the team whose map is being viewed is simply informed of or shown the location on the map. Players should try to make the spot difficult to reach from the map's starting point. After the players have given a treasure map location to an opposing team, they return to their own groups.

5. Distribute one sheet of letter-size paper to each team. Explain that the groups have five minutes to *write step-by-step directions* relating how to go from the starting point to the location of the treasure (which was determined in step 4) on their team's map. It should be emphasized that the clearer the instructions, the better the team's possibility of winning. Stop group work when the five-minute time period has elapsed.

6. The treasure hunters return and stand before their own team's map. One player from that team will read the directions to the "hunter." As the directions are being read, the hunter traces a line on the map according to the verbal instructions. The team whose hunter reaches the treasure first wins.

Discussion

♦ What type of information helped the treasure hunters the most? (*Use of details, compass directions, etc.*)

♦ What kind of information was the least helpful?

♦ How did planning the map and writing the directions relate to communication effectiveness?

♦ Relate this game to planning and communication in the workplace.

49 ◆ Twisters

Objective

To enter into a team competition launching paper helicopters at a target.

Applications

- ◆ Change
- ◆ Decision Making
- ◆ Goals
- ◆ Problem Solving
- ◆ Team Effort

Group Size

Six to thirty participants, who will work in teams of three to four members each.

Time Required

Twenty to forty-five minutes.

Materials

A poster board target; an index card, several sheets of blank paper, paper clips, a ruler, scissors, and a felt-tip marker for each participating team; one copy of the Twisters Handout for each participant; one copy of the Twisters Scoring Sheet for the facilitator; masking tape; a clock or timer; a flip chart.

Preparation

Duplicate one copy of the Twisters Handout for each participant. Make one copy of the Twisters Scoring Sheet for the facilitator. Obtain the following set of materials *for each participating team*: several sheets of blank paper (at least one for each team member), paper clips, a ruler, scissors, an index card, and a felt-tip marker. Using the poster board, prepare a target by drawing four concentric circles of 2", 4", 7", and 10". Label the target with the point system shown below:

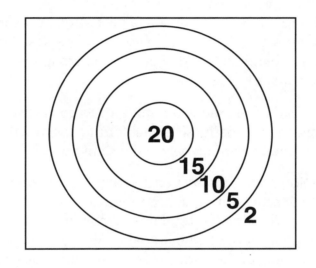

Place the target on the floor and use masking tape to mark a starting line approximately five to six feet away, with sufficient space behind the target for participants to throw their twisters.

Process

1. Instruct participants to form at least two teams of three to four members each. Distribute one copy of the Twisters Handout to each participant. Also provide each team with one set of materials (see Preparation step above). Assign a team number (or some other designation, such as a color) to each group for identifi-

cation purposes and put the team designations on your copy of the Twisters Scoring Sheet.

2. Explain that each participant will construct one "twister" to be entered into competition for his or her team. The Twisters Handout provides general guidelines on how to construct the paper "twister," but alterations may be made to the basic design. Indicate the competition set-up and describe the rules below.

> During competition, players will stand at the indicated starting line and throw their "twisters" toward the target in an attempt to receive the highest point score. (Refer to the target and explain the point system.) Each player will be allowed three tries, with the single best attempt recorded for the team's scoring. The team score will be based on the average number of points earned after *all* group members have participated.

3. Explain that teams will have exactly ten minutes to construct and test their twister entries *before* the competition. Signal for the construction phase to begin, and provide a one-minute warning before the time expires.

4. After the construction phase, instruct each team to estimate the total number of points it thinks it will score during the competition. Each group should write its team identification and estimated total score on an index card (cards were included in the original set of team materials). Allow several minutes for team discussion and recording of the anticipated score, then collect all the cards.

5. Conduct the competition, with all the players from each team taking their turns before the next team participates. Record each score (each team member's highest score out of three tries), then add up the team members' final scores and calculate the average Team Score (the average number of points) for each group using the Twisters Scoring Sheet. Referring to the previously collected index cards and the Scoring Sheet, use the flip chart to display the team estimates and the actual team scores for each group. Review this information with the participants and announce the team with the highest team score and the team that best predicted its final results.

Discussion

♦ How realistic were your team's goals?

♦ What influenced your team's final estimate?

♦ How many versions of the twisters did your team experiment with?

♦ Which versions did your team use for the actual competition?

♦ How did your team decide on which versions to use?

♦ How does this game relate to workplace situations regarding goal setting? problem solving? reengineering efforts?

Twisters Handout

INSTRUCTIONS:

1) Cut on the two middle horizontal lines and fold in.
2) Fold the bottom flap up.
3) Cut the vertical line at the top to create two flaps.
4) Attach a paper clip to the bottom.
5) Drop and watch spin!

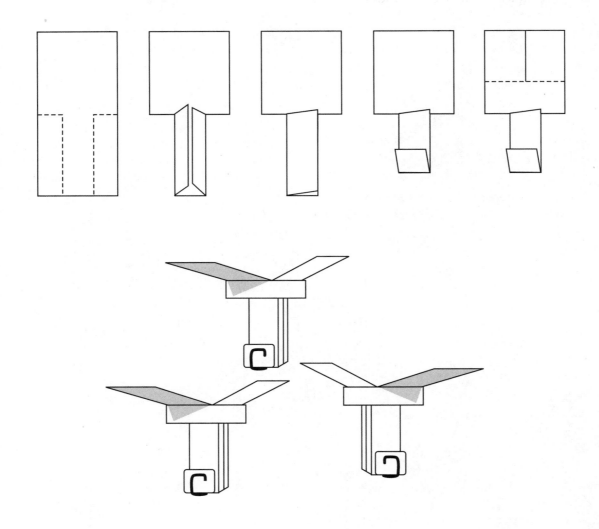

Twisters Scoring Sheet

TEAM I.D.	TEAM PLAYERS				Total Player Points	TEAM SCORE (Avg.)
	#1	#2	#3	#4		

50 ◆ Unbelievable!

Objective

To determine as a group which of three subject statements is false on a sheet of unbelievable "facts."

Applications

- ◆ Conflict Resolution
- ◆ Data Analysis
- ◆ Decision Making
- ◆ Icebreaker
- ◆ Time Pressure

Group Size

Unlimited. Participants will work in teams of up to five members each.

Time Required

Approximately ten minutes.

Materials

A pencil and one copy of the Unbelievable! Worksheet for each participant; a clock or timer.

Process

1. Instruct participants to form teams of up to five members each. Distribute a pencil and one copy of the Unbelievable! Worksheet to each participant. Read the instructions at the top of the worksheet. Stress that team members should discuss the statements and come to a consensus on the one statement in each set that is **False.** Teams will have exactly five minutes to complete the worksheet.

2. Signal for the groups to begin working together on the worksheets. Give a one-minute warning before the time expires.

3. Obtain feedback from teams on the answers to each question. Ask for some reasons why teams chose the statement that they did; check for different answers/reasons from other teams. Reveal the correct answer for each topic set, using the information provided below.

Solution

1. **b** (16 *moons*)

2. **c** (*totally false*)

3. **c** (*totally false*)

4. **a** (*blue laws forbid sale of ice cream sodas on Sunday*)

5. **a** (*Charles Strite; Westinghouse invented railway car air brake*)

6. **c** (*"golden means"*)

7. **b** (*Pearl S. Buck is her real name; she never used a pseudonym*)

Discussion

♦ What criteria did your team use in determining which statement was the false one?

♦ How were conflicts resolved?

♦ What are some ways in which we can check the accuracy of information we obtain? (*e.g., check a variety of sources, be aware of inconsistencies.*)

♦ How does time pressure affect our use of data in the workplace?

Unbelievable! Worksheet

Each topic below contains two TRUE statements and one that is FALSE. Your team is to select the statement that you think is FALSE.

1. a) It would take 17 years for a 747 jumbo jet to get from the Earth to the Sun.
   b) Jupiter has a total of 8 moons orbiting it.
   c) On Venus, a day lasts the equivalent of 243 Earth days.

2. a) During a 4-day eating marathon held by the Duke of Burgundy in the 15th Century, 28 musicians performed inside a giant pie.
   b) A London gentleman held an equine feast in 1864 which served horse consomme, horse liver, and a roast filet of Pegasus.
   c) In 1833, President Andrew Jackson had a banquet catered by the Iroquois Indians which included 20,000 pieces of chicken wings, 3,000 ears of corn-on-the-cob, and 5,000 sticky buns.

3. a) Hurricanes in Australia are called "willy-willies."
   b) An "umiak" is an Eskimo boat made of skins stretched on a wooden frame.
   c) The mask used by actors in ancient Greek drama plays is called a "trakhus."

4. a) The ice cream sundae originated because fountain owners received ice cream fresh from local dairies on Mondays, and on preceding Sundays they got rid of last week's leftovers by serving combinations of random flavors topped with syrup, fruit and nuts.
   b) The Good Humor ice cream brand was so named because the founder, Harry Burt, believed that "the humors of the mind are regulated by the palate."
   c) The ice cream brand *Frusen Gladje* means "frozen delight" in Swedish.

5. a) The pop-up toaster was invented by George Westinghouse.
   b) The inventor of the electric razor was Jacob Schick.
   c) Rudolf Diesel invented the diesel engine.

6. a) *Doppelganger* is German for "phantom double."
   b) *Beau geste* is French for "noble gesture."
   c) *Aurea mediocritas* is Latin for "inferior quality."

7. a) Eric Arthur Blair used the pen name George Orwell when he wrote *Animal Farm* and 1984.
   b) The real name of Pearl S. Buck, who wrote *The Good Earth*, was Camille Buccacio.
   c) L. Frank Baum, author of *The Wonderful Wizard of Oz*, also wrote under the pseudonym Edith Van Dyne.

51 ♦ Weak Link

Objective

To combine links for a paper chain tug-of-war.

Applications

♦ Change

♦ Decision Making

♦ Diversity

♦ Risk Taking

♦ Team Effort

Group Size

Unlimited. Participants will work in teams of five members each.

Time Required

Fifteen to forty minutes.

Materials

Ten 8½" × 5½" sheets of colored paper for each team, with each team's set designated by a different color; a stapler for each team; scissors.

Preparation

For each team, use five sheets of colored paper (each team should be given a different color of paper). Cut each sheet into halves (8½" × 5½" each).

Process

1. Instruct participants to form teams of five members each. Distribute a stapler and one set of ten paper sheets (half sheets) to each group, assigning one specific color to each team.

2. Explain that the teams will be competing in a paper chain tug-of-war. Each team member will construct one open link from a single half sheet of paper. During competition, the link will be looped through another team's link and attached using only one staple per link. Link strength will be tested by pulling the entire chain. Each team is permitted to have only one link entered into competition at any time. Groups have been supplied with enough paper to allow each member to make a practice link before constructing one for entry. Teams must decide the order in which links will be introduced into competition. Explain that the competition itself will be conducted as follows:

   (1) The representative from one team will begin the chain by creating a link, using one staple.

   (2) The player from the next team will bring an open link to the competition site, loop it through the first link, then close it using one staple.

   (3) This procedure is repeated until all teams have entered *one link each*.

   (4) Assign one participant to each end of the chain and have them both pull until one or more links break.

   (5) Any broken link is then replaced by another one from the appropriate team, identified by its color.

   (6) The competition continues for a set period of time (determined by the facilitator), with the winning team being the one with the most links left, or until only one team's link is remaining.

3. Announce that teams will have approximately ten minutes to design and construct their links, then signal for the construction phase of the activity to begin. Give a three-minute warning before the time expires, stopping group work when appropriate.

4. Conduct the competition according to the preceding directions, and continue until the time limit has expired or until only the winning team's link is remaining. Announce the winning team.

Discussion

♦ How did team members choose a construction method for their links?

♦ Was it necessary to adjust any original designs? Why?

♦ How did the team decide which paper link to use each time?

♦ In what way did each individual contribute to his or her team's overall performance?

♦ How can we relate this game to activities in the workplace?

52 ♦ Weather or Not

Objective

To use group decision-making skills in determining the validity of different weather-related trivia statements.

Applications

- ♦ Conflict Resolution

- ♦ Data Analysis

- ♦ Decision Making

- ♦ Leadership

Group Size

Unlimited. Participants will work in teams of five or six members each.

Time Required

Ten to twenty minutes.

Materials

A pencil and one copy of the Weather or Not Worksheet for each participant; a copy of the Weather or Not Answer Sheet; a flip chart; a felt-tip marker.

Process

1. Instruct participants to form a minimum of two teams of five or six members each. Distribute a pencil and one copy of the Weather or Not Worksheet to each

participant. Each team is to select one member to act as its leader. Assign a team number to each group.

2. Explain that members of each team are to discuss each of the statements provided on the Weather or Not Worksheet and to determine whether it is true or false. Each group leader is responsible for facilitating the decision-making process, resolving conflicts, and recording the team's answers.

3. Allow approximately five to ten minutes for teams to complete the group work and then signal for the activity to end.

4. Using the flip chart, record each team's answers next to the appropriate question. Review the answers using the information on the Weather or Not Answer Sheet. After each answer is revealed, score the team responses on the flip chart. The team with the most correct answers is the winner.

Discussion

♦ Did your team do better or worse than you expected?

♦ How did the team decide whether a statement was true or false?

♦ How did team leaders feel about their responsibilities?

♦ How were conflicts resolved?

♦ How confident of its answers was your team as the responses from other groups were recorded? Why?

♦ What factors can influence the effectiveness of the overall decision-making process? (*e.g. data, time, communication, group size, organizational climate, leadership*),

♦ How can teams work toward making more effective decisions in the workplace?

Weather or Not Worksheet

T   F   1. St. Petersburg, Florida could be considered the "brightest" place in the U.S., with a record 768 consecutive sunny days.

T   F   2. The state with the most tornadoes recorded in any one year is Kansas with a total of 182.

T   F   3. The highest temperature recorded for Verkhoyansk in Siberia was 98°F.

T   F   4. Commonwealth Bay in Antarctica is the world's windiest place with gales reaching 200 mph.

T   F   5. The most intense drought occurring in the U.S. lasted a total of 57 months in western Kansas.

T   F   6. The wettest state in the U.S. is Washington with an annual rainfall of 56 inches.

T   F   7. In January of 1943, the town of Spearfish in South Dakota experienced a temperature increase of 48 degrees in a span of only 2 minutes.

T   F   8. In March 1911, Tomarac, California set the record for the greatest depth of snow on the ground with a total of 37 feet 7 inches.

T   F   9. The state with the greatest number of deaths caused by lightning is California.

T   F   10. Cape Disappointment, Washington is considered the "foggiest" place in the United States because it averages 187 days of heavy fog each year.

Weather or Not Answer Sheet

1. **TRUE**—February 9, 1967 to March 17, 1969

2. **FALSE**—Texas with 232 recorded tornadoes

3. **TRUE**

4. **TRUE**

5. **TRUE**—May 1952 until March 1957

6. **FALSE**—Louisiana with 56 inches

7. **TRUE**—January 22, 1943, went from $-4°F$ at 7:30 a.m. to 45°F by 7:32 a.m.

8. **TRUE**

9. **FALSE**—Florida with 313 deaths since 1959

10. **FALSE**—average of 2,552 hours, or 106 days, of heavy fog each year

53 ◆ What's My Line?

Objective

To determine occupations represented by torn directory advertisements.

Applications

◆ Data Analysis

◆ Perception

◆ Problem Solving

◆ Time Pressure

Group Size

Unlimited. Participants will work in teams of up to five members each.

Time Required

Five to ten minutes.

Materials

A pencil and one copy of the What's My Line? Handout for each participant.

Process

1. Instruct participants to form teams of up to five members each. Distribute a pencil and one copy of the What's My Line? Handout to each participant.

2. Explain that the handout contains torn advertisements from a yellow pages telephone directory. Teams should use the information provided on the handout to determine each of the ten different occupations represented. When your team has agreed to all the occupations, group members are to rise and remain standing until all teams have completed the activity.

3. Signal for the activity to begin and allow approximately five minutes for the groups to work together (or until every team is finished). After everyone is standing, indicating completion of the exercise, ask participants to sit down and then review the correct answers using participant feedback and the solutions provided below.

Solution

(1) carpet cleaning   (6) roofing

(2) automobile repair   (7) travel agency

(3) dentistry   (8) prescription glasses

(4) pest control   (9) legal services

(5) podiatry   (10) pool maintenance

Discussion

♦ How did the display of teams standing when they were finished affect your team's approach to the task? Why?

♦ How difficult was this task? Why?

♦ What clues did your team use to solve the puzzles?

♦ What are some ways in which a business illustrates its "identity"? (*logos, slogans, themes, identifying colors, etc.*)

♦ How do individuals and/or teams display their personalities or character?

♦ What impact does individual perception have on this image?

What's My Line Handout

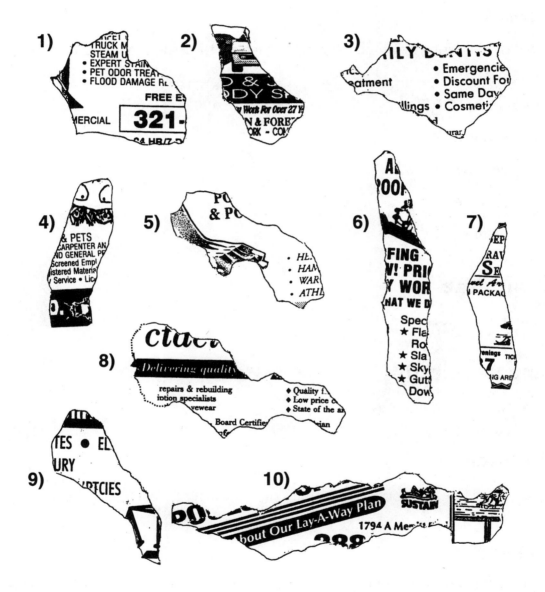

1) TRUCK M
STEAM U
• EXPERT STAIN
• PET ODOR TREA
• FLOOD DAMAGE Re
FREE E
MERCIAL 321-
HR/7 D

2) D & J
DY S
Work For Over 27 Y
N & FORE
ORK - CO

3) MILY D NTS
Emergencie
eatment • Discount For
• Same Day
llings • Cosmeti

4) & PETS
CARPENTER AN
ND GENERAL P
Screened Empl
istered Materia
Service • Lic

5) PO
& PO
• HE.
• HAM
• WAR
• ATH

6) A
OOF
FING
W! PRI
Y WOR
HAT WE D
Spec
★ Fla
Ro
★ Sla
★ Sky
★ Gutt
Dow

7) EP
RAV
SE
PACKA
enings TIC
7
G ARE

8) ctae
Delivering quality
repairs & rebuilding ♦ Quality
iotion specialists ♦ Low price
yewear ♦ State of the a
Board Certifie ian

9) TES • EL
URY
RTCIES

10) PO
out Our Lay-A-Way Plan SUSTAIN
1794 A Me t
288

54 ◆ Wordsmithing

Objective

To build on existing beginning and ending letters to create the longest word.

Applications

- ◆ Communication
- ◆ Decision Making
- ◆ Group Interaction
- ◆ Leadership

Group Size

Unlimited. Participants will work in teams of up to five members each.

Time Required

Approximately ten minutes.

Materials

A pencil and one copy of the Wordsmithing Worksheet for each participant.

Preparation

You have been provided one Wordsmithing Worksheet as well as a blank grid for creating customized worksheets. To use the grid, determine a word containing at least six but no more than ten letters. Print the word from top to bottom in the left-hand column and from bottom to top in the right-hand column of the grid.

Process

1. Instruct participants to form a minimum of two teams of up to five members each. Each team should select one group member to act as its team recorder.

2. Distribute a pencil and one copy of the Wordsmithing Worksheet to each participant. Explain that the teams will use the worksheet to attempt to fill in the space between each set of letters in the left-hand and right-hand columns with the *longest* possible word. *No proper names are allowed.* Each letter of the word formed per line results in one point; the two letters in the right and left columns are not counted in the score.

3. Provide the following example:

> If the letters presented had a first line beginning with the letter "P" and ending in the letter "L," adding the letters to spell "PRESIDENTIAL" would result in a score of 10 for that line. If letters had been added to spell the word "PARTIAL," a score of 5 would result.

4. Signal for the activity to begin, allowing approximately five minutes for group work. When this phase is completed, have each team score the total number of letters added and give its total to you. The team with the highest total score is the winner. If you wish, you may obtain feedback on some of the words derived for each set of letters.

Discussion

♦ How difficult was this game? Why?

♦ What problems, if any, did the leader encounter in regard to communication? decision making? group participation?

♦ How did the team decide on which words to use?

Wordsmithing Worksheet

			ADDED LETTERS
C		D	_____
R		E	_____
E		T	_____
A		A	_____
T		E	_____
E		R	_____
D		C	_____

TOTAL LETTERS ADDED: _____

Wordsmithing Custom Worksheet

TOTAL LETTERS ADDED: _____

55 ◆ Zoo Clue

Objective

To determine the proper sequence of different animals based on size without using verbal communication.

Applications

◆ Communication

◆ Decision Making

◆ Group Interaction

◆ Icebreaker

◆ Perception

◆ Problem Solving

Group Size

Eight to fifty participants, who will work in teams of eight to ten members each.

Time Required

Approximately ten minutes.

Materials

One set of Zoo Clue cards in an envelope for each participating team; a flip chart; a felt-tip marker.

Preparation

Duplicate the Zoo Clue Sheet on card stock, making one copy for each participating team. Cut each sheet into separate cards and place them in an envelope. You will need an envelope containing one set of cards for each participating team. Using the information given in the Solutions section below, write the names and approximate weights of the animals, in proper order, on the flip chart. Conceal the information from players until later in the activity.

Process

1. Instruct participants to form teams of approximately eight to ten members each. Assign each group to a different area of the room, allowing enough space between groups to allow for free movement and to enable each group to form a line. Distribute one envelope containing a set of cards to each team.

2. Explain that each team member will remove from the team's envelope one card that will assign the name of an animal to that player. Players are to keep these identities secret. On a signal from the facilitator, the team members are to line up in proper order, from the smallest to the largest animal, *without using any verbal communication*. Stress that *size should be determined by weight*, not height.

3. Signal for the activity to begin. After approximately five minutes, stop the teams and allow participants to reveal the animals they were representing by showing their cards to other members of their team. Explain that the teams may adjust their size sequencing if they desire before the correct order is revealed. Display the answers that were previously written on the flip chart and discuss with the groups.

Solution

(1) Rabbit	5-10 lbs.
(2) Fox	15 lbs.
(3) Anteater	35 lbs.
(4) Cheetah	100 lbs.
(5) Chimpanzee	150 lbs.

(6) Lion	350-550 lbs.
(7) Bear	1,500 lbs.
(8) Bison	2,000 lbs.
(9) Hippopotamus	3,000-9,000 lbs.
(10) Elephant	11,000-15,000 lbs.

Discussion

♦ How difficult was this task? Why?

♦ How does perception create false assumptions?

♦ After the identities of the animals were revealed, did the team need to make any adjustments to the order?

♦ How can we relate this game to problem solving and decision making in the workplace? (*share information openly, readjust as new data is available*).

Zoo Clue Sheet

RABBIT	**FOX**
ANTEATER	**CHIMPANZEE**
CHEETAH	**LION**
BEAR	**BISON**
HIPPOPOTAMUS	**ELEPHANT**

About the Author

Lorraine L. Ukens is the owner of Team-ing with Success, an organization specializing in team building and leadership development. Her wide range of business experience, spanning more than twenty years, is applied in designing, facilitating, and evaluating programs in a variety of training areas.

In 1993, Lorraine developed a comprehensive three-phase training program, also called **TEAM-ING WITH SUCCESS,**™ which was designed to help build and maintain high-performing teams. Since then, additional games and activities have been developed that use hands-on learning experiences to promote constructive group dynamics.

Lorraine received her M.S. degree in human resource development from Towson State University in Maryland. A writer and consultant, she is an active member of the American Society for Training and Development.